The Ageless Runner

To Glenn

Keep the running
going my friend

John

Diane Stone, Bill Welsh, Melva Murray, and Shirley Pettijohn at the NJ 8K Cross-Country Championships, 2016

The Ageless Runner

Keys to Their Success, Health, and Longevity

John Silver, PhD

Library of Congress Control Number: 2017909932

Book design by Gerry Burstein

Photographs by author

Cover photograph: Herman Bershtein, Jim Stevens, Janit Romayko, and Patty Carton at Docs Race, 2016

ISBN: 978-0-692-90058-1

Printed in the United States of America.
by
G&H SOHO, Inc.

*To my mother
who gave me the love and freedom
to blaze my own trail.*

Acknowledgments

There are several individuals I'd like to recognize for their assistance in making this book happen. First of all, I would like to thank Sheila Collins, retired political science professor, author, and friend, for her encouraging words and insightful ideas that helped me get the book off the ground. I would like to extend my gratitude to my good friend Dan Paget, retired professor of music and conductor, for his feedback and perceptive opinions which helped to further my vision for the manuscript. And I am grateful to my friend Bill Christophersen, former letters editor for Newsweek magazine, retired professor of literature, and author, who has done the copy-editing and assisted in revising ideas.

I would also like to thank my wife, Sara, who has carefully read the manuscript, offering astute impressions and constructive criticism along the way. And my mother, who is 92, deserves special recognition. I cannot thank her enough for her patience and thoughtfulness as I read her portions of the book over the phone, often on a daily basis, for the past year. Finally, I am indebted to the runners themselves, who opened their homes, their hearts, and their lives to me in making this book possible.

Contents

Introduction

W<small>E WERE OFF WITH THE SOUND OF THE GUN</small> at the Newport 10,000, a 10K (6.2 mile) race in downtown Jersey City. Just ahead of me was Tom, a fine older runner in his early 70s known for his short, quick strides and full head of flowing white hair. Slipping past him among the throngs of runners, I gave him a nod. Then suddenly someone came along on my left and bumped into me, yelling, "Hey, you're not supposed to be in this race, this is New Jersey, go back to New York." Immediately I recognized him as my racing nemesis, Nuno, a highly competitive runner who had recently turned 65 and was now in my age group. He is usually faster than I am, but his smacking into me and deriding me as an out-of-place New Yorker got my competitive juices going. I decided to see how long I could keep up with him, staying 10 to 20 yards in back of him, and letting him pace me. From behind, Nuno doesn't look like much of a runner. He's short, square and chunky. But don't let his physique fool you, this fellow can flat out run. There were times when he would put on a burst of speed and I would struggle to keep up, and each time we would turn a corner in the race he would be momentarily out of sight.

But being paced by Nuno and having him in my sights worked to my advantage. We made one final turn and there lay the Hudson River and the skyline of New York. After traversing five miles of twisting and turning Jersey City streets, the sight of that gleaming skyline, bathed in the late morning light, momentarily took my breath away. Getting my first glimpse of these majestic buildings, I remembered that this was my city, a city where I'd lived for 20 years, and a nostalgia came over me. Then Nuno's words came rushing back, stoking my competitive flame once again. He was in front of me by 20 yards or so when I decided to make my move. Approaching the boardwalk, I passed him in a spurt so he wouldn't get any notion that he was going to catch me. Soon I saw a sign for the five-mile marker and knew there was a little over a mile to the finish line. Running on that wooden walkway in full view of the river and skyline inspired me to give it my all, and occasionally I glanced over my shoulder to see if there was any sign of Nuno. There wasn't.

The Newport 10,000 is well known by competitive runners in the tri-state region and was advertised as a New Jersey State Championship 10K. After the race most of us mingled and conversed and found the refreshment table with plenty of orange slices, bananas, and pizza. The result board indicated that I'd come in third in my age group, which was exciting. Unfortunately for Nuno, he came in fourth and was out of contention for a medal. At the awards ceremony I picked up my third place medal for the 65-to-69 age group and chatted with Tom who had come in first in the 70-to-74 division. Later on while exiting the race site, I struck up a conversation with Nat Finestone, a rather tall, stocky fellow, and discovered he'd come in first in his age group at 86. Now that was impressive. Here is a guy running in a 6.2 mile race at 86, and keeping up an exceptional pace, given his age. When I asked him what the key to his success was, he stated that it was doing long training runs. It turns out that Nat also competes in half marathons.

Meeting older runners at these races and listening to their stories got me thinking about writing this book. Take Tony Medeiros, for example. We met at the Fairfield 5K in Connecticut in 2013, when Tony was 82. He revealed how he'd had triple bypass surgery and a pacemaker implanted a decade earlier. He also described having had partial knee replacement several years later—surgery that ultimately helped him return to running and competing in races. Hearing other amazing stories like Tony's intrigued me, and I thought they were worth documenting. These older runners, I suspected, had something to say about health and longevity that would be of interest to the public.

Beginning in October of 2015, I set out to capture these fascinating running histories, and completed all but a few of the interviews by February of 2016. That four-month journey in my Prius took me throughout the tri-state region from central and southern Connecticut to New Jersey to several locations in and around New York City. The recorded interviews generally took place in the runners' homes and lasted between one and two hours, with additional time spent photographing the runners and peering through albums, articles, personal records, and other related materials.

This book is based on those interviews with 34 older runners in their late 60s, 70s, 80s, and several in their 90s. It is astonishing that nearly all of these men and women are still running and competing in races. How, I wondered, have they been able to sustain such athletic endurance well into their later life? What is it about this particular group of athletes that sets them apart from most of their peers? These are among the questions this book attempts to answer.

It's Never Too Late

MY FIRST LOVE WAS BASKETBALL. Growing up in the Chicago suburbs, I had a hoop over the garage door and spent countless hours perfecting my shot. But it wasn't until going to college at the University of Wisconsin in Madison that I played with any regularity. The outside courts between the Ogg and Selery dorms are where my skills were developed, at least on the days I wasn't out demonstrating against the Vietnam War and getting tear gassed. Even now I have a passion for the sport and find myself on the court nearly every day in the winter months, shooting around and playing in pickup games. I'm no spring chicken at 67, but I'm hanging in there pretty well with the young whippersnappers. My jump shot is still my weapon of choice, and my running helps to build my endurance and keeps me fit on the defensive end. At 5'10" and 140 pounds, I don't have a big, bruising body to bang with, so I've learned to play an outside game to protect myself.

After college I began a 12-year career in jewelry making and photography, selling my work as a street artist and at art-and-craft fairs all over the Midwest. I also worked politically to expand vending rights and outside space for artists in Madison, and worked on the Mall Operating Committee as the artists' representative to help rewrite the ordinances on vending. There were many Christmas seasons in December when a group of us local artists would sit outside on the mall in front of the University Book Store selling our work.

4

One December in 1983, the coldest on record, I remember sitting huddled in my down sleeping bag day after day with a sign in front of me that read "10 degrees-below-zero sale."

Soon after Christmas, I would travel to Central and South America replenishing my jewelry materials and taking photographs of nature, wildlife, the Mayan and Incan ruins, and indigenous cultures. My jewelry made use of attractive seashells, which I collected on the West Coast of Mexico and learned how to drill, and of beads I made out of a variety of exotic wood from around the world, including cocobolo, zebra wood, East Indian and Brazilian rosewood, and ebony, which was so dense it would literally smoke when cut with a band saw.

Athletics, and especially basketball, were built into my next career. After moving from Madison to New York City in my late 30s, I went back to school for a master's degree in social work. For the next 20 years, working in inner city neighborhoods like Bedford Stuyvesant and Flatbush in Brooklyn and Belmont in the Bronx gave me a chance to carve out a special niche for myself. Including athletics within the therapy session proved to be an excellent engagement tool for working with African-American and Hispanic youth. Although we always talked first about whatever issues or problems were present, my clients then got to pick an activity and often chose a sport they liked. At PS 335 in Bed-Stuy, my office was the size of a classroom and empty of student desks, making it possible for several sports to be featured during therapy. One was an invented tennis game whereby my own desk would be moved to the middle of the room to act as the net and a rubber ball was hit back and forth over the desk using small paddles. Another was throwing the football, and one time we even had a 2-on-2 football game in the room.

But the activity my clients chose most often was basketball. I got very good at learning how to lose in order to help build their self-esteem. I still use this basketball technique today, purposely missing shots by hitting the front, back, or sides of the rim. Luckily, wherever I went in my social work career, the agency or school usually had access to a basketball court, and if not I would put up my small office hoop and push the furniture out of the way, and we'd play a rousing game of one-on-one or Horse. Many a day I would come home sweaty and tired from the physical activity. Even where I work today at the Therapy Center in Bedford Hills, N.Y., we have a basketball court out back. No doubt my youthful clients have helped to keep me physically active through my 40s, 50s and now into my 60s.

In addition to working with children, adolescents, and adults as a mental health therapist, I studied and received my Ph.D. in social work from Columbia University and taught in their master's in social work program. However, it was my work with youth in some of the toughest neighborhoods in Brooklyn and the Bronx that was the most gratifying, and incorporating sports made it especially memorable.

Having played in pick-up basketball games all my life, at 56 I joined a recreational league. After playing with this group for five years, one day I went down hard on the court after smashing into a blind screen, a powerfully built African-American fellow who outweighed me by a good 100 pounds. Staggering and dizzy and a little frightened, I made my way to the side of the court and sat down to collect myself. After regaining my equilibrium, I left the court and headed home wondering if this was the end of my basketball playing days.

Soon after that incident, my wife, Sara, saw a sign for a 5K (3.1 mile) race in FDR Park in our hometown of Yorktown Heights and suggested I give it a try. Running was always a little boring to me, but at 60 I began training for the first running race of my life. It was already May and the race was in early June, so there was little time to prepare, but I began practicing on the quarter-mile track in Yorktown. Well, coming in third in the 60s age group and winning an award in my race debut was so exciting that I was immediately hooked on the sport.

Following the purchase of my first pair of running shoes, my training became more routine and disciplined to better prepare me for the remainder of the racing season, which included another 5K, 10K, half marathon, and a swim/run biathlon. For the next four years I continued to compete in running races, but also in many swim/bike/run competitions known as triathlons. Not having ridden a bike since my early 20s, it was quite a challenge to get back in the saddle, and learn how to ride with a focus on speed and how to lock my bike shoes in and out of the pedals without falling. Yes, it's a bit scary, and of course everyone falls while learning how to do this. Then there was swimming. When first starting out, I could barely swim free style, also known as the crawl, from one end of the pool to the other, but within several months I was swimming a mile nonstop and only occasionally using the breaststroke for a breather. By the end of my second season in triathlon I finished off the year by participating in Toughman in Croton on Hudson, N.Y., a half-Ironman race with a 1.2-mile swim, 56 miles on the bike, and a half marathon run. At 63, I was the second-oldest in the race of over 500 participants, and collecting my third-place plaque and Ironman wristwatch was a proud achievement, even though there were only four in my age group.

After falling off my bike a couple of years ago and tearing the labrum in my right shoulder during a training ride, I decided to stop doing triathlons and concentrate on my running. This would give me a chance to see if my running and racing could improve. It certainly did. At age 65, my personal best times were set in the 4-miler, 5-miler, 10K, and half marathon, placing in all these races in my age group. It was particularly gratifying to run the 4-miler in 7:25/mile and the half marathon in 8:21/mile. However, by focusing just on the run, I aggravated an old hamstring injury. Is there something to be said for the benefits of cross-training and not using the same muscle groups over and over? We'll see what the older runners have to say about this and many other subjects on aging and athletics.

Richard Bleecker at the Cranford 4-miler, 2016

Richard Bleecker, 77

Ran a Race in
283 Consecutive Months

T HE STREAK WAS ON THE LINE. It was the final weekend in February, and a huge snow storm had come up the night before the 5K race at City Park in Bayonne, N.J. Close to a foot of snow had blanketed the region, but that morning Richard and his wife, Juanita, drove down with great difficulty only to find the race site deserted. Finally, with only minutes before the official start to the race, Francisco, an officer of the club sponsoring the event, showed up. Richard explained to him that if the race wasn't run he'd lose his monthly streak, and Francisco suggested they call the club president for clarification on whether the race could be run. Richard was able to reach this fellow by phone. "The three of us are here," Richard said. "We have paid our money; we know the course; if we run the race and clock ourselves, and report our times, will it please count as an official race?" The club president said, "Sure." There had been no plowing done in the park, the snow was nearly up to their knees, and they wore face masks to protect themselves from the pelting snowflakes and wind. Bounding through the mounds of snow, the three of them ran the race and then went for coffee and breakfast. The monthly streak had been in the making for five years. "That was a close call," says Richard.

9

Richard had run a race in every month since December, 1992, but by the beginning of 2015 the streak appeared to be over. Chronic pain in his right hip made running an ordeal, and Richard knew he could not go on. "I knew that surgery was inevitable, either that or a lifetime of debilitation and pain," he said. Seeking the advice of two surgeons, he was confronted with a diagnosis of osteoarthritis of the hips. Both doctors confirmed the need for hip replacement surgery using the traditional posterior cut method with a minimum of two to six months of rehabilitation. And both physicians told him he should never run again. But Richard didn't give up. He continued to research medical websites and make calls until he found two surgeons who were conducting an updated version of the operation, using the anterior cut technique. Their prognosis sounded slightly less dire, but they nonetheless advised a minimum of two months of rehab and forbid running.

Once again, Richard went back to the drawing board, and this time came upon a new medical technique. The superior cut method had, at the time, been performed for less than a year by only four surgeons in North America. It was a micro-procedure that did not damage vital, healthy tissue, and the surgeon, Dr. Brandon Gough, assured Richard that he would make a quick recovery. In the doctor's words, "You need to wait about six weeks, carefully think about doing any more marathons, and don't try out for the Olympics. And of course you can run again."

Richard was delighted. To keep his streak alive, he scheduled the surgery for February 2nd. He ran a 5K race in Tempe, Arizona, on February 1st. The next day he had the operation. Then he recuperated for seven weeks, and followed up with another 5K in Gilbert, Arizona, on March 21st. The operation had succeeded and the racing streak—and Richards running career—had been saved.

I met Richard at the Firecracker 4-Miler in Cranford, N.J., on July 4th, 2015, five months after his hip surgery, and he was still running at a 12:00/mile pace. In the months leading up to the surgery, running had been very painful, but since the operation, Richard has been free of discomfort in the hip and his racing times have steadily improved. Even the minor discomfort in his left hip and knees has been reduced, which Richard attributes to the correction in his alignment and ability to run more naturally.

Running a Race in All 50 States

After running in a race or two in nearby states for several years, Richard and his wife, Juanita, got the idea of completing a race in all 50 states. Being retired and having the time, they bought a small RV and traveled throughout the continental U.S., visiting and racing in three to six states each trip (of course they flew to Alaska and Hawaii). Richard illustrates their final journey in this way:

> Upon our return from Hawaii we set off in our RV on an extended trip through the American Southwest. The trip lasted two and a half months, covering 10,000 miles and featured visits to eight national parks and three presidential museums. Along the way we ran races in California, Colorado, Mississippi, Oklahoma, and Utah. Our objective was achieved on May 18 (2008), as we ran the Steps to the Cure 5K in Overland Park, Kansas, our 50th state.

It took Richard and Juanita approximately a decade—from 1998 to 2008—to accomplish their goal of running a race in every state. It was a great way to see the country and view its natural beauty.

Richard Bleecker was born on July 26, 1939, in Newton, N.J. Facing a challenging early childhood with the loss of his father at four and his mother struggling to care for her two children, Richard left home to attend a boarding school from fourth to sixth grade. With the remarriage of his mother, he returned home to his family, a new stepfather, and a more normal upbringing. Despite these youthful hardships, Richard went on to receive his doctorate in education and to lead a distinguished career. He states:

> My Ed.D. (University of Arizona) took me to the next level in a career devoted to improving our complicated and crowded planet by helping those in need. For a quarter century, I specialized in service to blind and visually handicapped persons and blindness prevention. . . . For my last hurrah, I spent a decade as the founding exec-

utive director of a not-for-profit organization specializing in substance abuse prevention.

Richard had two children, went through a traumatic divorce, and in 1976, moved to his present home in Jersey City, N.J. He says he was overweight, was "smoking and drinking immoderately," and was in need of a lifestyle change. As he puts it, "I reorganized my life priorities and began to pay more attention to my health." For a start, Richard quit smoking, cut back on drinking, focused on eating healthier meals, and began swimming and light jogging. Within a few years, Richard met and married Juanita, his current wife.

Thus, a long and fruitful running career was launched. Starting in his mid-30s, Richard continued his jogging unabated for eight years until his first 5K race in 1984, which he describes as a "transforming and liberating experience." After that competition he was hooked on racing. Richard has run in 476 road races, averaging about 15 events a year. At the end of his first competitive season he prepared for and ran his first marathon, and he completed eight marathons in his first eight years of racing, when he was between the ages of 44 and 52. He ran his fastest marathon in a respectable 3 hours and 44 minutes (3:44). Following these strenuous races, Richard thought it best to save his body and hold off on any more marathons. It was then, in 1992, that he began his monthly racing streak.

But a decade later, his wife caught the marathon bug and decided she wanted to celebrate her 50th birthday by running the New York City Marathon in 2002. Although Richard couldn't get into that marathon, to support Juanita he signed up for another so they could train together, and he ran that 26.2 mile race at the age of 63. The next year they ran the New York City Marathon together. Then in 2004, as Richard states, "We ran the New York City Marathon again and finished hand-in-hand with smiles on our faces," crossing the finish line together in 5:46. He was 65 at the time. Five years later, Richard decided to celebrate his turning 70 with a marathon. This time he and his wife ran the Philadelphia Marathon. Richard finished 30 seconds ahead of Juanita in 5:36. He says, "She was closing fast, according to her."

Keys to Richard's Success, Health, and Longevity

Richard attributes part of his success in running to his wife, Juanita. As he points out, "I had the good luck of being married to a woman who shares similar interests in health and fitness." Juanita has been a continuous running companion for over three decades, sharing in training runs and going to the races. Richard also notes, "We've made a lot of dietary modifications." These include eating more organic foods, largely giving up soda and sugar, eating less red meat, and eating few desserts.

Richard emphasizes that his training and exercise regimen has evolved. He started out just jogging for many years, and, once he began racing, his training focused almost exclusively on running. Yet, over the years, Richard began to incorporate some light weight training and use of the elliptical and stationary bike, all of which have been integrated into his current regimen. He now limits running to once or twice a week for about an hour, and wears a Fitbit to count his steps. He looks to reach 10,000 steps a day, which corresponds to walking about four miles. After dinner, instead of collapsing on the couch, he will often go out for a walk to meet his daily step requisite. Richard believes a further reason for his success is having a goal to work toward. Running a race in every state and maintaining his current monthly race streak have kept him focused on his training and being physically active. This has also helped him to stay at a healthy weight below 160 pounds.

When asked how long his monthly racing streak was likely to last, Richard replied: "In an ideal world, I'll live to be 100 and maintain reasonably good health, and given those predicates, I see no reason why I can't keep this streak going for 24 more years."

Bill Tribou, 2015

Bill Tribou, 96

Ran the Mile in 4:14
Ranked 11th in the World

IT WAS 1942, and as a senior at the University of Connecticut, Bill was preparing for the race of his life. The track coach, Ivan Fuqua, a former gold medal Olympian for the U.S., entered Bill in the IC4A, Eastern college championships on Randall's Island, N.Y., featuring some of the best milers in the country. The following is Bill's recollection of that race:

> The gun went off, and I ran my regular first quarter, and I was with a group of five or six of us up there toward the front. When we went by the quarter mile I heard the time, but to me it felt like I was running slow to keep up with those four or five of us up there, so I put on a little speed and I went in the lead of this group, which included Les McMitchell, who was probably the best miler in the country at the time. I went through the half mile leading that group, and then I still felt great. What the hell, I'll keep going. I don't care what they're doing, I'm ahead of them. And now we had one lap to go, and I'm leading the god-damn race. I can't believe it. And I'm feeling good, my legs felt good . . . And with only about 100 yards left I thought, Jesus, I'm going to win this race, and I couldn't believe it. But then McMitchell came by me with maybe 60 yards to go, and now my legs were gone and I was sprinting like hell. McMitchell passed me so now I'm second and then, who the hell, oh, Don

Burnham from Dartmouth passed me, and then Bill Holtz from New York passed me, and, Jesus, but I'm running as fast as I can now and I only got 20 yards to go, and so, well, I got fourth place anyway. But my time was 4:14, and that was good time in those days.

Television had not yet been invented, but the race had been on the radio, and Bill called his father who said, "Wow, you had quite a race down there." Bill's official time in the mile was clocked at 4 minutes and 14.7 seconds, and it certainly was a good time in 1942, good enough to rank Mr. Tribou 11th in the world. The world record at the time was 4:04, and it would be another 12 years before the four-minute mile barrier would be broken by Roger Bannister in 1954. And keep in mind Bill was a 94-year-old man during the time of this interview reminiscing in vivid detail about a race that took place over 70 years ago.

Bill Tribou was born in Hampden Highlands, Maine on December 18, 1920. He moved with his family to Connecticut, and as a sophomore at Wethersfield High School, he started out on the soccer team but wasn't very good. One day, as Bill was leaving the classroom, his history teacher, Mr. Carlton, yelled, "Tribou, you've got long legs, I want you to try out for my track team." And Bill thought to himself, "Well, I'm not doing very well in history, maybe if I go out for his team, you know. . . ."

Bill joined the track team as a sophomore but didn't do well that first year. Yet, by his junior year he'd won all the races in his signature event—the mile. The big race that year was the Hartford Mile, with all the best high-school milers in the area competing. Bill describes the race:

And I'll be god-damned if it was just one of those days when you're a runner when everything went right and I won the race. We were three of us coming down the home stretch, and this was the first time I really had a battle . . . and I stuck out my chest at the finish line and just nicked the tape before the other two guys, but when I stuck out my chest I was leaning forward and I fell straight down on the cinders.

This was all very exciting for Bill who says, "When I fell down but won the race, the next morning the *(Hartford) Courant* printed it on the front sports page. . . . After that race I was a runner, that's all I can say."

After high school, Bill moved on to the University of Connecticut, where he had an esteemed career as an All-American runner and an elite miler. He graduated from UConn in 1942 and, with World War Two raging, went into the armed forces that October. Having been in Rotary Officers Training Camp, ROTC, Bill was inducted into the army as a second lieutenant and sent to the city of Oran, a big U.S. military port in present-day Algeria, where he was stationed for two and a half years loading and unloading military ships.

The Race Through Mers el Kebir

While Bill was in Oran, a recreational director, Zeke Bonura, an ex-Major League baseball player who was known for his home run power with the Chicago White Sox, organized a five-mile race, and 18 military personnel signed up, including Bill. Along the route was the town of Mers el Kebir, a naval anchorage known as the Great Harbor, where President Roosevelt had met General Eisenhower and Admiral Cunningham, the British commander-in-chief of the Mediterranean, in 1943 to discuss military strategy for North Africa. Bill portrays the race as follows:

> After Mers el Kebir we drove up into the mountains. So Zeke got up this big mountain, and he stopped at the top, and he said, "Get out, this is where we are going to start". . . . We all looked at each other, and I said, "Where are we going to race, down the mountain here?" He said, "Yea, we're going to run down the mountain, through Mers el Kebir, and then up to Oran, and finish on the main street of Oran". . . . And I thought, Christ, we're going to race down a mountain? So I thought, what the hell, I'll jog down the mountain, and so I did and took it easy. And I didn't hear anyone around me after a mile, so I turned around and looked back and could hardly see a guy way back there. So I jogged past Mers el Kebir . . . And we only had about a mile to go when we got into this tunnel, and Zeke must have had 50 motor cycles around us so nobody would

kill us. Well, I barely made it out of the tunnel. I thought I was going to pass out with all the gas, you know.

Bill won the race and received his first-place trophy, a brace anti-aircraft shell especially engraved for him. After the war's conclusion, Bill joined a track team the army had created, which traveled throughout Europe putting on races to entertain the troops until there were enough ships to take them back to the States.

With the war over and the troops home, Bill returned to Connecticut, got a job with Travelers Insurance Company, married Marjory, and had two sons. With work and family life intruding, he took a break from competing for about 20 years, but remained physically active by playing a lot of golf and jogging after coming home from work. By the time Bill was in his mid-40s, his kids were grown and he was back to serious training and racing. His routine consisted of running three to five miles a day, five to six days a week, unless he was preparing for a marathon, and in that case he would increase his daily mileage. Bill estimates in his running career—which spanned nearly eight decades—that he ran over 2000 races and, more often than not, won his age group. He competed in about 20 marathons, mostly in his 50s and 60s, including six Boston Marathons. Bill has a plaque on his living room wall depicting his first Boston Marathon in 1975, which he ran in 3 hours and 2 minutes (3:02) at 54 years of age. Yet the 5-miler, and later the 5K, when it became the most popular race, were always his favorite events.

National Runner of the Year Five Times in His Late-80s and Early-90s

What is unique about Bill Tribou is that he was an elite competitor throughout his running history, but especially as a young man and, 60 years later, as a man in his 80s and 90s. In the 4.75 mile Manchester Road Race, one of the premier events in the Northeast, Bill still holds the course records in the 80-84, 85-89, and 90-plus age groups. In the 5K distance Bill has won numerous awards at national and Senior Games championships. The USA Track & Field, the organization that chooses and trains our Olympic team, bestowed upon Bill the Runner of the Year award in his age group five times when he was 85, 86, 90, 92 and 93. At 90, he ran 23 races and was still running in the 11:00/mile range. Bill is undoubtedly one of the finest 90-year-old distance runners of all time.

At 93 years of age Bill ran seven races. Then at 94 he tried running a 5K on New Year's Day, 2015, but could only manage to run a mile and a half of the race, and at that point he knew it was time to call it quits. With a touch of sadness Bill reflects, "Once I stopped running, it seemed like a big chunk of my life was gone. . . . I miss it horribly." Bill also misses his running buddies. There was a group of about 14 couples that would meet at the races and go out for lunch afterwards, and he says, "I'm the only one left from the original group. That's what happens when you live to 94."

Thankfully, Bill has family in the area. His two sons are not in the vicinity, but his second wife, Nancy, had five children of her own, and they all still live in the area. Although Bill has been living alone in the house since Nancy's death six years ago, he often gets together with his five step-children and their many children and grandchildren, as well as a few of the "younger" runners he is still in touch with. He has lunch out of the house nearly every day and has a fondness for attending to the flower pots and two birdfeeders in the yard.

Keys to Bill's Success, Health, and Longevity

Bill flatly states that he has been "lucky" and hasn't done anything in particular to deserve special recognition. Yet he does say, "I have taken good care of myself, never been a heavy drinker, and eaten healthy all my life." One of the most important factors for Bill's durability in the sport of running has been the camaraderie. Much of his social life was built around the weekend races and all the runners and their wives he knew. He points out that his first wife, Marjory, and Nancy were both very supportive of his running, would attend all his races, and were a part of that social fabric.

Being injury free is an essential component for Bill's health in road racing. Amazingly, he had only one major medical setback over the course of his 80 years of running, and that was the removal of his appendix back in his senior year in high school. He credits his moderate workouts and not over-training with helping him remain free of injuries. Another key to Bill's success as a runner was the competition itself, which he adored. Once the race commenced, his competitive spirit was ignited and he ran to triumph over all runners in his age group.

Lastly, running and racing gave Bill purpose in his life. "It gave me something to do," he says, "and I was good at it."

Monica Roche, 77
Fortitude and the Fortuitous Fall

Monica had a fondness for running in foreign countries, but there were times the natives were less than hospitable. She recalls one such occasion:

> I went to China in December of 1979 for three weeks. . . . Of course they weren't used to Westerners, and I remember one man fell off his bike because he was staring so hard. Another time, we arrived in Nanking, and I ran onto a military base. I ran past a guard, and I think I woke him up because he was absolutely furious, and he's got this big rifle and he's shouting at me, and so I turned around and ran in the opposite direction. Well, by that time the army was out running, and they're in my way, and I'm thinking, is it illegal to run past the army? But I just put my head down and went past them.

Monica Roche was born on March 19, 1939, in Pelham, N.Y. After graduating from college, she obtained a master's degree in nursing from New York Medical College, which led to a satisfying career as a nurse. She worked for nearly a half century, before retiring at 74. At age 35, while working at New York Cornell Hospital in New York City and living in Manhattan, she started running. Monica explains how it happened:

> I stuck myself with a needle from a patient who was Hepatitis B Positive. So as usual you bleed it, and you pour bleach on it, and you

Monica Roche, 2015

do all this kind of stuff. At that time we had to get a shot of gamma globulin, 5-CCs in each buttock, and I was told this was going to be very painful and horrible. So the best thing to do was to go and jog after you get the injection, so it wouldn't hurt. And actually it was not a bad idea, because you're so stiff from running, which you're not used to doing, you don't feel the shot. Then, a month later I had to get the shot again, and I ran again. And the second time, I thought, this is kind of fun. So I took up running.

Monica began by running just a mile after work for a few years and then, with the encouragement of a colleague, built up to three miles. In 1978, when Monica was 39, she joined the New York Road Runners club, began entering races, and, within a couple of years, entered her first New York City Marathon, which she completed in 3:44, at 8:33/mile, her personal best time for a marathon. Monica reflects on that first of six New York City marathons: "I thoroughly enjoyed it because you're running through all these neighborhoods. In fact, I met a couple from Alaska, and they'd never been East before, and they decided to come and run the New York City Marathon, and it was the greatest way to see the city."

Monica's other personal best times are equally impressive. For instance, she ran a half marathon in 1:41, at 7:45/mile, and a five-miler in 35:07 at close to 7:00/mile. She believes she ran about 35 half marathons, which was her favorite distance, until she had back surgery at 50 and began to compete only in the shorter events. Monica estimates that she ran 10 to 15 races a year while living in New York City, but in the past decade she has turned up the volume, averaging closer to 35 races a year, and, overall, has totaled more than 500 competitions.

For Monica, running had an extra benefit. It was a way to deal with the anger and frustration as a nurse over the years, and she expresses it in this way:

After work, if I'd had a really rough day, I would run just about as far as I could. I remember one time I just kept running and running, and I found myself down in the Bowery and the bums are looking up at me. I didn't really think about where I was going or for how long. . . . Sometimes I pretended I was running across the faces of all the people I was mad at.

The Fall

Within the past decade, Monica has taken four significant falls on her face. She points out, "I do not lose consciousness, but I do not seem to catch myself, and that is the scary thing." Monica reports that the first three falls didn't stop her from running for more than a couple of weeks, and, luckily, didn't result in anything more than cuts and bruises and a trip to urgent care. But in May of 2015 the fourth fall was different:

> I was running along happily. I was only a quarter of a mile from the finish, and I landed really hard, wham, right over the eye here (pointing). Here (pointing) my teeth were not quite in the right place. I said, "How far are we from the finish?" They said, "A quarter of a mile." I said, "I'll keep going." So I got up, I'm not kidding, and I limped to the end. We get a little nutty, I think. And I looked a mess. I was bleeding here, here, and here (pointing). "The ambulance will meet you at the end," they said. So I get there and the ambulance isn't there. After I fell, another woman fell and broke her arm, and the ambulance took her to the hospital. So I drove all the way home to Fairfield and directly to urgent care. They took a look at me and they wanted to take me immediately to the hospital. So I had to go in an ambulance.

They took Monica to St. Vincent's Hospital in Bridgeport, Conn., for a cat scan of the head, neck, and cervical spine, which were all OK. But the knee had been fractured, so she had to wear a large black knee support. After physical therapy she improved quickly, and she was back walking three miles several times a week by the time of this interview. But when asked about the future, Monica was frank: "I don't think I want to run in a race. I might jog a little by myself, but not in a race. When I think about falling, I get a chill. I'm still having trouble with my teeth, and I've spent $5000 so far."

On January 1, 2016, at the Chilly/Chili 5K in Orange, Conn., two months after my interview with Monica, there she was, to my amazement, crossing the finish line in a respectable 37:28, at 12:04/mile. Monica had recovered swiftly, had faced her fears, and was back to racing.

Keys to Monica's Success, Health, and Longevity

Monica thinks it's crucial not to over-train. She states, "Knowing when to back off is important. Certainly, knowing what you can do and can't do, and not trying to do too much is the key." Reading books on running, Monica believes, has helped her gain understanding and guidance in the sport. She notes too that her eating habits have evolved over the years. She says, "I try to eat healthy, but the stuff I read about how they make hamburgers and what they do to chickens—I don't want steroids or antibiotics." So Monica instead prefers pasta, cheeses, fruit, vegetables, salads, fish, and lots of sweets.

A final reflection from Monica: "I guess I never had an injury persistent and painful enough to stop me."

Walter Desind, 2015

Walter Desind, 85

Cancer Survivor and Still Racing

In his 60s, Walter displayed his gritty determination:

> I did the Rockland County Marathon on January 3rd. It was three degrees below zero, and 13 degrees below zero wind-chill. The drinking water froze. The race was a mile out and a mile back, back and forth 12 times. At the four-hour mark I had 22 miles. When I got back at the starting point after 24 miles, the fellas at the timing table said, "Here's your medal, we're going home. Call me when you finish the race and give me your finishing time." I finished the race, called them up, and gave them the time. It was freezing and we had no water. Anyway, that was a memorable marathon.

Walter Desind was born on May 8, 1931, in Brooklyn, N.Y. When his son was 16 and on the high-school track team, he said to himself, "If my son can run, why can't I?" Soon Walter was off and running. From age 52 to 85 he has competed in over 500 races, including 15 marathons and 22 triathlons. One of his highlights was placing first in the New Jersey Masters Championship 5K, in 2006, in 25:54, at 8:22/mile, at age 75. Walter's final marathon was the New York City Marathon two months after the 9/11—World Trade Center attack. He was 70, and looking back, he says, "When the group of us were running, every time we saw a cop or fireman, everybody gave a loud cheer."

Then, on September 11, 2002, Walter had prostate surgery. He has been cancer free ever since, and it's become a motivating force: "That's another reason why I want to run now. . . . I'm better than you, cancer. I beat you, you son of a gun, I beat you."

Walter worked for ABC, CBS, and NBC as a film editor beginning in the 1950s, and retired 30 years later in his mid-50s. He has three sons, and has been married for 63 years. I originally met Walter as he was looking for his car after the Norwood, N.J., 5K, in 2014. I offered to help, and we finally located Walter's vehicle. It was then that he began to reveal his running history. But Walter wasn't the only older runner I met that day. After the race, I conversed with this fellow, Bob Pettie, who had beaten Walter and come in first in the 80+ age group. Bob was 86 years of age and racing with a fully-replaced knee. These miraculous running stories were registering in my mind, and my ideas for the book were beginning to coalesce.

Keys to Walter's Success, Health and Longevity

A major key for Walter is his conviction not to quit. He says, "I'm going to run until I die, until I cannot do it anymore, until I can't get out of bed. I'm going to walk, race, and run."

A few final words from Walter: "It's like the Nike ad, Just Do It. In the morning, I don't want to get up, I don't want to go out. I simply say, get your ass out of bed and go."

Julio Aguirre, 70

Fastest Man His Age in New York City Area

AT 54 YEARS OF AGE Julio hit his peak, but, admittedly, he didn't always run smart. It was the Las Vegas Marathon of 2000, and Julio takes us to the race and teaches us a lesson:

> I can tell you, I was running with this girl. She's from Romania. And I don't like girls beating me, so I was pushing and tried to beat her. When we crossed the half marathon, our time was 1:20. So I said, "Too fast, definitely too fast." So when we get to mile 23, I hit the wall, and she's gone, and she finished with 2:42 and I finished in 2:54, and I walked the last 5K.

This is a lesson that many runners learn the hard way, as Julio did in this race. He confessed that he should not have let her dictate his pace, but, rather, he needed to pace himself and run his own race. Yet, what is extraordinary about Julio's performance in this marathon is his time of 2:54, considering the fact that he had to walk much of the last three miles.

Cigarettes, Alcohol, and Gambling

Addictions were dominating Julio's existence. The ensuing financial and health risks were creating a downward spiral and damaging his personal life, he notes:

Julio Aguirre at Cranford 4-miler, 2016

When I came to the United States, besides working, I started drinking, I smoked cigarettes a lot, and played cards for money. I used to lose all my money playing cards, and I would get drunk every weekend. My life was a complete disaster. . . . I had a problem at home because I had no money and that was the cause of my divorce.

Then came the epiphany that transformed his life:

One day I was in Central Park drinking with friends overnight. About 9 o'clock in the morning I saw a race, and I talked to my friends about running in high school, and they were laughing at me saying, "Julio, you're only good for drinking, not for running." When I got home I thought, "Why not start running again? I have some ability in that."

Julio started running and he hasn't looked back. Around that time, he completely changed his lifestyle, gave up smoking and gambling entirely, and cut back on his drinking to a couple of beers, eventually giving up alcohol altogether. Now, on occasion, he will have a drink socially.

Julio Aguirre was born on June 16, 1946, in Milagro, Ecuador. He worked as a math teacher and an accountant in his home country before coming to the United States when he was 31 years of age. Once in the U.S., he had steady employment working in a factory, but had trouble controlling his addictions, and his first wife walked out on him, taking their three children. By age 46, however, running had afforded Julio a new lease on life, and he turned himself around.

For nearly a quarter century, Julio has proved to be one of the finest competitive runners his age in the Tri-State region. He estimates he has competed in roughly 1500 races. In his 50s he was averaging about 100 races a year, and in his 60s close to 50 races a year. Some of Julio's racing stats are awe-inspiring: At age 53, Julio ran a 5K in Yorktown Heights, N.Y., in 17:29 at 5:38/mile, and a 10K in Prospect Park, Brooklyn, in 36:27 at 5:52/mile. At age 54, Julio ran the Staten Island Half Marathon in 1:19:41, and a month earlier he had run the Brooklyn Half Marathon in 1:20:46, both at 6:04/mile. Also at 54, he ran the Chicago Marathon in 2:52 at 6:34/mile. And Julio is particularly proud of running the Indianapolis Marathon in

3:12 at 7:20/mile, when he was 66. These race results are staggering, given Julio's age.

12-Time Winner of Runner of the Year Award

For his running prowess, Julio has been honored with perhaps the most-coveted road-racing award in the New York City region, the Runner of the Year, which is conferred by the New York Road Runners club. But Julio didn't just win the award once—he's won it 12 times. So far he has won the prize three times each in the 50-to-54, 55-to-59, and 60-to-64 age groups, twice for the 65-to-69 division, and once for the 70-to-74 category.

Long-distance running has always been Julio's forte. He has run approximately 200 half marathons, and his 60 marathons have taken place all over the world and in roughly 20 major cities of the U.S. Some of the notable marathons Julio has run include New York City (16 times), Boston, Berlin, Copenhagen, Belfast, Barcelona, Seville, Rio de Janeiro, San Blas in Puerto Rico, and Guayaquil in Ecuador. And Julio is well known in unexpected places. At the finish line in the Berlin Marathon, people knew him and were calling out his name. On another occasion at a race in Ohio, Julio was standing in line to get an autograph from Bill Rodgers, the four-time winner of the New York City and Boston Marathons, but security shut the line down at 4 p.m. While Julio was arguing with the security guards, Bill yelled out, "Hey Julio, come on over, I'll give you my autograph." Julio asked, "You know my name?" And Bill said, "Everybody knows you, Julio."

Defying the Odds and the Doctors

Julio was in his late 40s and training up to six miles a day when he heard he'd been accepted to his first New York City Marathon. Being eager and excited, Julio drastically increased his mileage, running 12 to 18 miles a day, but after a few weeks he was diagnosed with shin splints in both legs and could hardly walk. On a vacation to Ecuador, he went to see his doctor who told him emphatically not to run anymore. One day, nine months later, Julio started jogging and discovered that the shin splints had miraculously disappeared. Again, he was off and running.

In 2002 at 56 years of age, Julio was training hard, doing 400-meter intervals in 1:08 with 30-second recovery times and up to 12 repetitions. That's extremely taxing on the body. Julio admits, "But I was killing myself, I was going too fast." The day after one of these strenuous interval sessions, Julio was taken to the hospital in agony. On the floor of the emergency room and writhing in pain, he was yelling out, "Somebody help me." He recalls, "And the police come and say, 'This guy is dying. Why are you not taking care of him?'" Julio was finally transferred to Mt. Sinai Hospital and immediately went into surgery to dissolve a blood clot in his heart. He had suffered a heart attack. After the operation, he spent a week in the intensive-care unit and a second week in recovery at the hospital. Julio says he almost died.

The doctor's orders were swift and simple:

> When I got out of the hospital the doctor told me, "Forget about racing anymore. You can't run anymore." And they gave me medicine for life. . . . About four days after I got home from the hospital, I went to buy the newspaper and I was walking, and I started walking a little faster, and then I start jogging. And for about two weeks I was walking and jogging. Okay, you're going to be surprised. One month after that, I won the Bronx Half Marathon. . . . Some of the people at the race were surprised. They said, "Julio, why are you here?" Because everybody knew I had been in the hospital. They had put a notice on the internet, and everyone had been calling me.

Julio had defied the odds, the doctors, and even death to win the Bronx Half Marathon for his age group in 1:25 at 6:40/mile, only seven weeks after his heart attack and surgery. He was convinced, however, that the demanding interval work he'd been doing had created the clot in his heart, and as long as he avoided that kind of training he'd be alright.

At age 60 in 2006, Julio suffered a torn meniscus of the right knee. His orthopedist, Andrew Rosen, also a runner, diagnosed the problem and recommended arthroscopic repair. Julio tells us what happened next:

> He did my surgery, and he says, "Julio, please, you have to take care of your knee. At least for one month don't do anything." I say, "Okay." A week after that I can't stay home, and so I went out and start walking, and I get faster, and then I start jogging. Then, after another week of jogging, I have the Queens Half Marathon. I did it and won my division. But when I crossed the finish line, I fell and I had a lot of pain. It was because of my surgery. I did the half marathon with my stitches in. A year later I had to go again for the surgery.

Although Julio continued to run for the next year, his injured knee had compromised his ability to run and race. A year later he went back to the same surgeon and had the operation done again. The doctor said, "Now Julio, take a month." This time he took three weeks recovery, and apparently that was sufficient. Then, in 2012, Julio had a meniscus tear of the left knee and returned to Dr. Rosen for another arthroscopic surgery. As before, the doctor's advice was to take a month for recovery, but Julio, pushing the envelope, again took just three weeks, yet again with good results. He is one tough, resilient athlete. After a heart attack and follow-up operation, and three arthroscopic surgeries on his knees, Julio remains the top runner at age 70 in the Tri-State area.

Keys to Julio's Success, Health, and Longevity

Julio thinks that his training has been a primary reason he has thrived in the sport of road racing at his age. He continues to run five days a week, four to ten miles a day, and on the weekend will usually include a 12-to-15 mile easier run. A couple of days a week he will do a 6:00 a.m. speed run of four miles, and later in the day a moderately fast six-mile run. No doubt, Julio's dedication to his training is having the desired results. Another factor that Julio emphasizes is diet: "Now I eat healthy. Fish and chicken, no red meat, and fruit, a lot of fruit. I don't have dinner, I just have grapes." In fact, Julio will consume as much as one to two pounds of grapes in an evening and spends $25 to $30 a week on the fruit. Furthermore, by working at the Super Runners store for the past 15 years and coaching in the sport, Julio has been able to integrate his work and his passion for running. He believes this is another key to his success and longevity in road racing.

Advice from Julio: "Stay away from drugs, alcohol, and cigarettes. And exercise, that's the best for everyone."

Diane Stone, 2015

Diane Stone, 85

Four Decades of Running Injury Free

Over the years, Diane has received hundreds of trophies, plaques, and medals in her races. One award, however, was not what she expected. She recalls:

> The prize I won at one race was a gold cigarette lighter. It was from the American Bar and Grill in Georgetown, Washington. So I took it back to them and I said, "You know, runners really don't smoke." And they said, "Okay, our customers love it but we'll give you an umbrella instead."

Diane Stone was born on September 12, 1931, in Chester, N.J. One morning in her mid-40s, Diane joined a group of runners from her fitness club going out for a run, and she hasn't broken stride since. Although depicting herself as "a middle-of-the-pack runner all my life," Diane still had some rather speedy performances. Take, for example, the Cherry Blossom 10-Miler in Washington, D.C., back in 1978, where she ran the race in 86 minutes at close to 8:30/mile. She notes that Bill Rodgers, the legendary marathoner, was in the race and ran it in 48:57, at a pace of under 5:00/mile, and adds, "Last spring I ran with Bill again, 37 years later, at a 5K in Staten Island." In recent years Diane is especially enjoying her racing and friendships with Melva, Shirley, Pat, and Caroline, the other four women runners on her 80s team from the Morris County Striders. They like to go out for refreshments together after a race and take their fellow runner, Bill Welsh, age 87, with them.

For the past 40 years, Diane has run 35 to 40 races a year, totaling roughly 1400 competitions. In fact, even in 2015, at age 84, she entered 40 events. And what is truly remarkable is that somehow she has kept herself healthy and fit the past four decades without physical impairment. How has she been able to do this? Basically, Diane has run for pleasure and the fellowship with other runners, not for the competition or to be fast. As she puts it, "I've run injury free, and I think it's because I didn't push myself beyond what I was capable of doing. I'm not that competitive, and I want to keep it enjoyable."

Keys to Diane's Success, Health, and Longevity

Diane describes the primary key to her well-being: "It's kind of a spiritual thing, I would say, knowing where your energy, health, and ability comes from. It comes from God. . . . I guess I've just been blessed." Diane also believes that attitude is important. She describes herself as happy and says, "Feeling content and grateful, I think those are the two big things."

Diane was married to David for 52 years, adopted a son, Tim, and enjoyed her work in calligraphy. The last time I caught up with Diane was at the New Jersey 8K Championships in October of 2016, where she romped to victory in her age group.

A tip from Diane: "Enjoy the little things and be grateful for everything."

Ed Regner, 88
The Four Generation Race

Eᴅ ʜᴀs ᴀ ʜᴜᴍᴏʀᴏᴜs ᴛᴀʟᴇ about a fellow competitor:

There is a funny story about Herman Bershtein. We ran a race in Trumbull, Conn., I think it was a 5K. In previous races, he had been beating me almost every time. He'd stay right behind me, and then we'd get to the last 500 feet or so and he'd pour it on. After the race, he'd tell me, "That's how I beat you—you paced me." But this one race in Trumbull, I stayed right behind him all the way through the race. So I thought I'm going to pull a little trick on him. The last 200 feet I'm going to pour it on, and I'm going to beat him to the finish line. Well, we got maybe 500 to 800 feet from the finish line, and all of a sudden a wind came up and blew his hat off, and he had to stop and grab his hat. Well, I didn't slow down or anything, I just kept going. I didn't have to pour it on, he got slowed down to pick up his hat, and I beat him across the finish line. . . . Of course now I'm not competing in his age group anymore; he's 90 now.

Perhaps in this race with Herman providence intervened on Ed's behalf.

Ed Regner with photo of four generations of family members who ran the Madd Dash 5K with him on his 62nd anniversary, 2015

Ed Regner was born on July 25, 1928, in Torrington, Conn. To avoid the Korean War, after high school he enlisted in the navy. Ed explains, "The Korean conflict was going on, and they were drafting people, and I didn't want to be in the trenches in the army. I wanted to be in the navy, so I'd have a bunk on a ship wherever I was. And also I had a crazy reason. I was a good swimmer, and if the ship went down, I could still swim to safety." Ed flew in the naval air force off aircraft carriers, operating the radar in the back of the planes. They would cruise around the Mediterranean Sea practicing anti-aircraft and anti-submarine warfare in preparation for being sent to Korea. Fortunately for Ed, he was never sent.

After his naval discharge in 1951, Ed went to college on the GI Bill, graduated from the University of Connecticut in 1956 with a degree in electrical engineering, and landed a job in his home town of Torrington. Around that time he married Kathy, and they had four sons and began to raise their family.

Inspiration for running came later in life for Ed. As he remembers, "I began running for my health in March of 1968. I read an article in the Reader's Digest, Keys to Fitness at Any Age—The New Aerobics, by Kenneth Cooper." That article catalyzed Ed's interest in running, and using Cooper's statistical formula, he kept meticulous records of his training and racing for decades. At 40, Ed started running just one to two miles several times a week, but by the time he began competitive racing at 60, his mileage had increased to four to six miles about five days a week. Although Ed has primarily run for health and was never a particularly fast runner, he still has enjoyed attending the races. He reckons he has averaged 15 competitions a year for the past 28 years—about 400 races—and he has boxes of his trophies tucked away in the basement of his home as proof of his accomplishments. For many years, Ed ran the 20K New Haven Road Race, his longest event at 12.4 miles. Currently, at age 88, Ed's usual distance is the 5K, but his favorite event has always been the Litchfield Road Race, a 7-miler he still does every year. Ed continues to go out a couple times a week for his four-mile training runs, but he now jogs, and walks up the hills.

Racing with 13 Family Members
on His 62nd Anniversary

Ed and Kathy's 62nd wedding anniversary was coming up in August of 2015, and one of the grandchildren, Michelle, became the organizing force to bring the whole family together to celebrate the occasion and have everyone participate in a race. The 26th Annual Mad Dash 5K in Stratford, Conn., just happened to land conveniently on the day of the anniversary and was a favorite race Ed ran each year. The family responded enthusiastically. They all met for this momentous occasion, with everyone running in the race except Kathy, who became the designated cheerleader. The family members included Ed's four sons and three of their spouses, three grandchildren, and the two great-grandkids, Sebastian who was three years of age, better known as Sebbie, and Sadie, his sister, who was four. Ed had this to say about the great-grandkids in the race. "Sebbie's the one that didn't jog or run the whole race. He was pushed in a stroller and walked some of it, especially across the finish line. And Sadie, his sister was jogging and walking, jogging and walking the whole thing."

There were a total of 13 members of the Regner extended family that took part in this 5K race, representing four generations. Acknowledging such a rare occurrence, Ed pointed out, "Marty Schaivone (the race director) even said it was the first time in his career that he'd had four generations in a race." In tribute to the achievement, Ed and his family received an exquisite trophy with five running human figures adorning the prize.

Keys to Ed's Success, Health, and Longevity

Ed emphasizes that he has been active all his life, particularly running and doing yard work the past 60 years, and is a primary key to his health. But he postulates there may be another reason:

> I went to see my eye doctor a couple of years ago, and he sat on the stool and he looked a little puzzled. He asked, "How come your eyes are so damn good?" I said, "Well, there are two things I do that

not many people do. I run a lot, I run in a lot of races, and I donate blood, I donate blood about every 56 days." At the time I had my 21 gallon pin. I've got 22 gallons now and I'm working on my 23rd gallon. And the doctor said, "Maybe that could be why your eyes are so good. New blood being produced all the time and good circulation from the running."

By the way, Ed still mows his two acres of land on a riding lawn-mower and uses a hand mower for the trimming.

Gerry Burstein, 2016

Gerry Burstein, 77
Work and Hamstrings Intrude

At 75 YEARS OF AGE, Gerry had just completed the New York City Marathon for the sixth time. How he ever finds the opportunity to train for these long races is a wonder. He still works 13-hour days during the week from 5:00 a.m. to 6:30 p.m., and an additional half day on Saturdays at his own book printing company. The only reprieve from work is helping out with the grandkids a couple of late afternoons during the week. Soon after his marathon Gerry went to meet the kids, and here's what happened:

> So my wife and I pick up the grandchildren from daycare two days each a week. They're four and two. One time—I think it was the Tuesday after my last marathon—we both picked the kids up because we take them to this program where there is music and dancing for the kids, and the adults would also join in. The woman who was running it looked at me and said, "If you don't want to dance or do any of this, you don't have to; it might be a little strenuous." And my wife said, "He just finished running the marathon!"

Gerry Burstein was born on May 2, 1939, in Cranston, R.I. After graduating from the Carnegie Institute of Technology in 1961, he started his own business at a book-designing studio in 1971, and eventually transitioned to his current book-printing enterprise. He has been married to Lorraine for 45 years, and they have two children, Susanne and Jason. I had the pleasure of meeting this sleek and talented runner at the Tenafly, N.J., 5K race, where we sat together during the awards ceremony. Gerry had easily come in first in his age group in a speedy 9:02/mile pace.

When Gerry was 48 he was persuaded by some youths in an anti-drinking program in high school to run a local five-mile race. He attempted to convince some of the older folk to join in as well, but all the adults declined. That didn't deter Gerry, however, who ran this race, his very first, in a swift 35 minutes at a 7:00/mile pace, with little more than a month of training under his belt. It appeared that Gerry was a natural at the sport of running, but work and family were forever intruding on his time. For a while, nights became the only option for training. "I had two young kids," he says. "So I would get them ready for bed, read to them, get them in bed, and then go out for a run." By his late 50s, the kids were older and Gerry was able to steal more time for running. He entered his first New York City Marathon at 57, and ran a personal best in New York at age 60, in 3:37. Here is a gentleman of 60 coming in the top 15% of all runners in the largest and most competitive marathon in the world. Overall, he has completed at least 300 races in the past three decades, many of them in New York City with his daughter, Susanne, including his last two New York City Marathons at age 70 and 75.

Hamstring cramping had always hampered Gerry on his marathon quests. These painful contractions never occurred during other races or even on 20-mile training runs. But on marathon day, between mile 12 and 15, the hamstring spasms inevitably began their onslaught, and the 2003 New York City Marathon was no exception. Gerry takes us back in time:

> When you come back into the park for that last couple of hundred yards, it's just amazing. You've got the energy to finish, and you can see the banner. . . . But in 2003, I had all these hamstring problems. Right at the corner as you go onto 59th Street I pulled up again, and there was a volunteer standing there, and I said, "Let me lay down behind you, I need to stretch out." And at one point I had my eyes closed, and I look up and there are three cops standing over me and they ask, "Are you alright?" And I say, "Oh, yah yah, I'm fine, I

46

just had to stretch out." And I started to get up and they helped me, but they stood me up much too quickly, and the world spun, and I found myself flat on my back again. So they said, "Maybe we should call the wagon?" And I said, "Oh no! I just ran 25 miles to this point. There's no way I'm not going to finish the race." And then I said, "Okay, I'm good, I'm going to go finish." And the volunteer said, "You're not going to run anymore, are you? Promise me you're not going to run." So I said, "No, I won't." So I walked up to the entrance to the park and said, "Screw this," and took off and trotted in.

Keys to Gerry's Success, Health, and Longevity

Gerry was quite clear about the major key to his success, health, and longevity—the running. He says:

I have friends who are badly overweight and do no exercise, and I don't want to look like that. And I don't have the discipline to go to a gym. I have to run at my pace, when I can do it, and that's what I do to stay in shape. . . . It's also a release of tension. I'm pretty intense about work, and it gives me a chance to clear my head and think about things. And sometimes at the end of the run you think, boy I love this, this is great.

By the way, Gerry has no intention of retiring anytime soon, from running or working.

Janit Romayko, 2015

Janit Romayko, 71
Has Completed 3000 Races

DRESSING UP IN COSTUME, Janit and her husband, Jim, headed down to the Midnight Run, a five-mile race in Central Park offering champagne to the runners along the route. As Janit describes it:

> My favorite was the New Year's Eve race in New York City, where I dressed up as a champagne bottle . . . We were toasting along the way, and I don't know what my time was, but I'm sure I wasn't there for the time, I was there for the good time. And it was so festive to see confetti all over the streets.

Jim dressed up as the cork, but the costumes were heavy and cumbersome, and the hard part was walking back to Grand Central Station in the wee hours of the morning a bit hungover.

Janit had a fondness for dressing up in costume for races. For 25 consecutive years she and Jim ran a 3.5-mile race in Glastonbury, Conn., which was known for its group costume category. Janit joined the Silk City Striders, a running club based in Manchester, Conn., and they would all dress up in identical costumes for this race. The name Silk City Striders came from the Manchester mill that made silk for the construction of parachutes during World War Two. Janit designed and painted the costumes, and all her hard work paid off. The Silk City Striders would dress up as Santa's reindeer, Christmas cards, cellphones, gingerbread men, Christmas ornaments or Hershey's Kisses, and they won the group costume award most years they entered.

The Senior Olympics

At the Pittsburgh Senior Olympics in 2005, Janit's maternal aunt was smooth as velvet in the water as she took the gold medal in the 50-yard backstroke. She was 95 years of age. Janit entered the 100-yard and 200-yard breaststroke and came away with the bronze medal in each event in her age group. And Janit's mother, who competed in the 100-yard, 200-yard, and 500-yard freestyle at 91, medaled in her events. For two decades, from 1995 to 2005, Janit, her mother, and her aunt traveled to the Senior Games together. These national competitions were held every two years, and it was a time of special bonding for the three of them. Janit's mother past away in 2013, four months shy of her 100th birthday. She had been swimming just nine days before her death. Her aunt died 11 days before her 100th birthday. No doubt genetics plays a role in Janit's athleticism.

Run 169 Towns in Connecticut

Janit remembered, "Eight of us got together one day at Dunkin' Donuts and said, 'Let's do this,'" thus creating the idea of a running club with the goal of racing in all the towns of Connecticut. A town in the state must have a municipal government, and there are 169 such towns in Connecticut. The first official meeting of the club, Run 169 Towns Society, took place in New Briton, Conn., in 2011, where Janit took the minutes, followed by the creation of the by-laws and a website by the current President, Richard Zbrozek. At a 5K race in Beacon Falls, Conn., on October 11, 2015, Janit completed her 169th town. Karen Rogers was the first woman to race in all 169 towns, Janit was the second, and there have been four men who have completed the task. The club has grown from seven to eight individuals to having a membership of over 1000. As Janit reflects, "The good thing about this group is that there are no dues and it's non-competitive . . . We wanted to promote a healthy lifestyle for people, and it's been great because a lot of people have said this really has made a difference in their lives." Members of the club can often be recognized by their yellow and blue t-shirts at races all over Connecticut.

38 Consecutive Manchester Road Races and Then . . .

The streak was at 38 and counting for one of the most prestigious races in New England when Janit went down. This is her reflection upon that moment in time:

> I fell in the rain on marble, and I broke my kneecap. I was just coming out of a concert and I slipped, and it was one month before the Manchester Road Race. . . . Luckily, the orthopedic surgeon that I go to is also a runner, and he said to the physician assistant, "Put her in a brace; we don't have to put her in a cast. Put her in a brace for a month and tell her don't take it off." So I got out of the brace on a Monday, the race was on Thursday, and I had no muscle left. Luckily, the doctor's office was right at the pool where I also swim and I went right in the water and started kicking. So with the aid of swimming and strengthening my leg, I got to the race on Thursday, and I had to run and walk in the race and I had to wear my brace. . . . This was the Manchester. I was 67, and that was my 39th time, and I wasn't going to break my streak. If I was going to have to crawl, I was going to crawl.

This particular event was back in 2012, and Janit has now completed the Manchester Road Race 42 times in a row. Her grandmother took her to view this competition at four years of age, and even then she remembered there were no women in the race. By the early 1970s women were finally permitted to compete in the sport of running and road racing, around the time when Janit ran her first Manchester race.

46 Marathons

For nearly two decades in her 30s and 40s, Janit enjoyed the challenge of the marathon, running the Boston Marathon four times, the New

York City Marathon three times, the Long Island Marathon about 15 times, the Bermuda and Holyoke marathons multiple times, as well as many others. Her best performance was her very first at the East Lyme Marathon in Connecticut in 3:30. But to Janit there was nothing more breathtaking than her first New York City Marathon. She reminisces:

> I remember going across that bridge feeling like the thing is shaking because there were so many people. There were 30,000 that year, I think. And it was also a thrill because the crowds were there. It was one big crowd for 26.2 miles. And then coming around that corner from Central Park by mile 25 and hearing, I think, it's Frank Sinatra who sings New York, New York, that was, oh my god, I still get shivers thinking about it, what a thrill. . . . And coming into the park and coming to the finish line and seeing the balloons. Oh my god, I just did the New York Marathon. It was massive, it was one big party, one big everyone cheering for you.

Janit Romayko was born on July 2, 1945, in Manchester, Conn. Teaching as a profession did not appeal to Janit, so she went back to school for a master's in social work and found her calling. However, there was a great deal of tension related to her work, and that's where her running played a significant role. Janit points out, "Running for me was a good stress reliever, because, as you well know, you hear a lot of stories all day long, and your sense of reality gets to you. You broaden your horizons but at the same time deal with problems that are insurmountable, and I thought running relieved the stress." She continues to work part-time as a social worker, and has a Grandmothers Raising Grandchildren group she has coordinated since 1986.

Janit estimates competing in approximately 3000 races over a 40-year span. This sounded like a bit of a stretch, so I inquired further, and Janit explained that since the 1970s she has been racing most Saturdays and Sundays throughout the year, which corresponds to nearly 100 races a year for the past four decades. The total number of races also includes hundreds of triathlons, which she feels have complemented her road racing, and believes the cross-training has been healthy for her body. Her current training consists of going to the YMCA at 6:00 a.m. to swim for a half hour to an hour, coming home and taking the dog for a four-mile run, and in the evening taking the dog out for another four-mile run, which computes to putting in 40 miles of running each week. Janit points out that she does not train on the bike, but gets her cycling workouts during the triathlons.

Currently, Janit is a member of four running clubs, including the Hartford Track Club, The Silk City Striders, Run 169 Towns Society, and the New England 65+ Runners. Since the death of her husband in 2011, she relies even more on the relationships that have grown out of her devotion to the sports of running and triathlon. When asked what running and racing have meant to her, Janit responded, "I think it's been a big part of my life. It's kept me going. It gave me a goal, it gave me a purpose, it gave me meaning, it gave me new friendships."

The Keys to Janit's Success, Health, and Longevity

Good genes certainly are a consideration. With her mother competing nationally as a swimmer into her 90s and living to 99, and her father, who had been a minor league pitcher at one time and lived to 96, it's no surprise that Janit should inherit a robust constitution. She also reports that her daily routine of running, swimming, and getting enough sleep is a key to her racing success and overall health. Finally, she credits the support of her husband, Jim, a partner who shared in the excitement and passion of running and the races until his passing five years ago.

A tip from Janit: "Find something you would like to do that's physical and do it."

Sid Skolnick at the Chilly Chili Run, 2016. His bib number reflects his age.

Sid Skolnick, 91
Still Running, Biking, and Swimming

YOU HAD TO DECIDE whether you were doing the 5K or 10k. Sid registered for the 5K, but while running, he got distracted by talking to the guys who were all doing the 10K. As Sid remembers, "I didn't even see the turnoff for the 5K. So we're running along, and I said, 'This is an awfully long 5K.' They said, 'You're not running the 5K, you're running the 10K.'" This was the first time Sid had ever run that far, but he managed to do just fine.

At 40 years of age, Sid started running with a group that called themselves the Sleeping Giant Pacers, named after a local state park that encircled a mountain whose face looked like a sleeping giant. Soon, Sid joined his fellow club members at the races, and they would all pile in their cars and drive there together. But he was not interested in the dates and times of his races. "I was never competitive," he says. "I was just happy to finish the race. I was a social runner, I wasn't a competitive runner." And yet, Sid was no slouch either. He ran the New Haven 20K, a 12.4 mile race, in under 100 minutes, cracking the 8:00/mile pace. For the past half century, Sid reckons he has competed in about 1000 races, his favorite being the New Haven 20K, which he has run some 20 times. I had the pleasure to catch up with Sid at the 5K Docs Race in June of 2016, where he came in first in his age division, ahead of his two 90-year-old rivals, Herman Bershtein and Don Osborne.

Sid Skolnick was born on December, 2, 1925, in New Haven, Conn. In 1943, with World War Two raging, he enlisted in the Army Air Corp at 17 and was training for combat on the B24 as a nose-gunner, with the expectation of being sent to the Pacific arena. Fortunately, the war ended and he was never sent. After starting out his career as an elementary school teacher and principal, Sid earned his Ph.D. in education and taught reading and research at Southern Connecticut State University and the University of Connecticut. He was married for a short time but soon divorced and confesses, "I found out I wasn't the best marriage material, but I always had girlfriends."

By the time Sid was in his 40s and teaching at Southern, his physical exploits were many and varied. Running four to five days a week was simply a piece of the mosaic. Sid explains, "All of the years I was running and teaching, I was doing a Wednesday bike ride of 30 miles on the Farmington Canal, and I swam a mile every day at Southern doing laps in the pool." Sid was also the faculty sponsor of the annual school triathlon, an event he participated in 12 consecutive years. But that's not all. Sid volunteered with the Appalachian Mountain Club as a camp leader on month-long hiking and climbing excursions from Mt. Rainier to Glacier National Park, and he has climbed all the major Eastern peaks from Mt. Washington in New Hampshire to Mt. Marcy in the Adirondacks. Sid says, "I was doing this as a volunteer and leading groups, so I had to be in pretty good shape." Besides these strenuous adventures, Sid volunteered for trail maintenance in Alaska and helped map trails in one of the Virgin Islands.

Keys to Sid's Success, Health, and Longevity

Genetics may have enhanced Sid's physical abilities. His mother died of old age at 104. But the fundamental key to his success, health, and longevity, he believes, has been his participation in a variety of physical endeavors. As Sid points out, "Looking back, I can see I was injury free because of cross-training. I think it helps your endurance and helps you to be free of injuries. I was using all my muscles." As of this interview in January of 2016, Sid, at age 90, holds to this tenet. He alternates running and race-walking up to five miles every other day, swims for an hour at the pool in his retirement home on days he doesn't run, and still goes out on 30-mile bike rides once a week, although not in the winter. And yet, what is most astonishing is that Sid has been able to sustain his athletic prowess while suffering from a form of chronic leukemia since his mid-70s.

Some advice from Sid:

> Sitting in one place all day long is a good way to shorten your life. Getting up off your ass and moving your body in any way you enjoy, whether it's roller-blading, skiing, or whatever, is the key. Your body was meant to work, genetically and historically. The old adage, "Use it or lose it," is true. You just got to keep moving. I don't even like sitting down like this for very long. If I go to a movie here, there's a place where I can sit without being seen, and I do exercises while I'm watching the movie.

Hank Schiffman, 2015

Hank Schiffman, 67

Fastest Runner His Age in New York City Region

Oₙ ᴀ Sᴀᴛᴜʀᴅᴀʏ ᴍᴏʀɴɪɴɢ ɪɴ Jᴜɴᴇ, The Race to the Clouds, better known as the Mount Washington Road Race, has a feared reputation. Hank is an elite age-group runner, but the 4700 vertical climb takes a toll on all competitors. However, that didn't stop Hank, who, after this punishing 7.6-mile run up the mountainside, got in his car and was off to the next event, the Whiteface Mountain Uphill Bike Race, some 150 miles away. By 5:00 p.m., he was on his road bike and ascending the 11 miles to the finish line. And that's not all. Then, Hank got back in his car, drove 300 miles back to New York City, got a few hours of sleep, and was off to Central Park for a five-mile race. Hank sums it up by saying, "So within 24 hours I'd run up Mount Washington, cycled up Whiteface, and run the five miles in the city." Sounds pretty crazy, but it demonstrates what Hank describes as his aerobic fitness.

Hank Schiffman was born on August 9, 1949, in Brooklyn, N.Y. He ran in high school as a senior and in college as a freshman, but he says he was very slow and gave it up. By age 30 he returned to running, but only for pleasure and fitness, until knee pain sidelined him in his early 40s. Hank remembers, "The doctor said, 'Sit down,' and he shook my knee and said, 'You have chondromalacia; you're running days are over.' And so I gave up running." Hank took up cycling at this time, and would go to Central Park and do three laps—25 miles around the park—before going to work.

Then, a decade later in 2000, at age 53, Hank tried running again, and, miraculously, the knee condition had somehow resolved itself. With renewed vigor he plunged into the sport, joined a running team, and learned the skills and nuances of road racing. Hank has now matured into one of the finest masters runners his age in the country. He won the acclaimed New York Road Runners club, Runner of the Year award for his age group for 2015, and again for 2016. His racing times are noteworthy. Hank has run the New York City Marathon 10 times, and in 2013 at age 64, he ran it in 3:27, at 7:54/mile. At age 61 he ran the Scotland Run 10K in 39:57, at 6:26/mile, and at age 65 he ran the Brooklyn Half Marathon in 1:33, at 7:06/mile, coming in first out of 63 runners in his age group.

Keys to Hank's Success, Health, and Longevity

Hank describes his keys as follows:

> The general public doesn't understand the importance of maintaining fitness. That's the key, maintaining aerobic fitness. It will help to ward off chronic diseases and it will keep you biologically younger than your chronological age. . . . And injury prevention is a key. Here's my rule of thumb. I start running, and if I feel something is not right, I turn around and walk home. If I feel it the next day, I won't run for a week. . . . Also, I think another key to my success is I have the ability to suffer. Because when you are out racing, you are uncomfortable. You're pushing your body beyond what its comfort limit is. When you're competing, you have to push yourself as far as you can, so you have to have the ability to take it, to take the punishment. Some people are not willing to push themselves out of their comfort zone.

Hank graduated from the New York University School of Dentistry with a Doctor of Dental Surgery degree and has worked as an endodontist specializing in root canal treatment for 35 years. He has been joyfully married to Georgia for 30 years. (Just in case you're wondering how I met Hank, he's my endodontist.)

A few final words from Hank:

> There is a thing about Zen. Less analysis but more being. It's all about being. So you want to be the cat jumping on the table. When the cat jumps on the table, it doesn't consider this, it doesn't consider that, it just jumps on the table. When I'm skiing, when I'm running, when I'm cycling, I just lose myself. And I feel I'm fulfilling what I am, that's the sense of being alive.

Melva Murray, 2015

Melva Murray, 84
Racing with Two Replaced Hips

BACK IN 1992, Melva and her daughter, Erynn, had the privilege to run with two of the most influential road-racing legends of all time, the great marathoner, Grete Waitz, and Fred Lebow. Melva describes this memorable encounter as follows:

> It was in the New York City Marathon, and we were in Fred Lebow's army, and he and Grete had a lot of people around them, so we stayed with this group of runners. Fred had had a brain tumor, and this was after he had his brain surgery. They were just 10 feet away from us, and we were running side by side with them for 11 miles. I finally dropped back and went to an Advil station, because they had Advil stations back then.

Grete was a nine-time winner of the New York City Marathon and former world record holder in that distance whose life was cut short by cancer, and who died in 2011 at 57 years of age. Fred was the co-founder of the New York City Marathon and its race director, while conjointly being president of the New York Road Runners (NYRR) club for 22 years until his death from brain cancer in 1994 at age 62. Melva had the privilege to run for a couple of hours with these two giants of running history in the very event they helped to mold into the leading marathon in the world today. Sadly, they were both taken from us in the prime of their lives.

Melva Murray was born on July 14, 1932, in the Bronx, N.Y. In her childhood she was always physically active:

> My father was handball champion runner-up in the city of New York in 1940, and I used to get all his dead handballs, and we'd go out and play. We didn't have electronics. We didn't sit in front of the television or iPhone or iPad. I rode my bike, roller-skated, and took dancing lessons for seven years in tap, toe, and ballet, and I've ice-skated all my life.

Out of high school, Melva worked for five years as a professional dancer, and soon after as a dental assistant, along with doing office work for six years. Then, as she and her husband, Cortland, raised their two daughters, Erynn and Robyn, Melva stayed at home for the next 13 years before joining American Cyanamid in Wayne, N.J., as an order processor, where she remained for the next 20 years. While at Cyanamid, she routinely worked out at the office fitness center, taking aerobic classes and using the stair-master, rowing machine, and other types of apparatus.

With Erynn providing the inspiration, Melva took up running when she was 50, and they would run together at the Wayne Valley track. About two years later they began doing 5Ks and 10Ks together, and around this time Melva also joined the Cyanamid running team and started racing with them in New York City. Soon she was fraternizing with a host of running clubs and became enamored with the sport of road racing.

On average, Melva has competed in about 40 races a year from the time she was 52 until the present, and estimates running in over 1000 races in her career, from the mile to the marathon. She took a short break from running at 62 for about three years when she lost her job at Cyanamid, along with her running partners, her house, and her will to compete. But she bounced back and, with renewed vigor and new running friendships, carried on her love for the sport.

The marathon was Melva's preferred distance, completing nine New York City Marathons and one Marine Corp Marathon. She said, "Hey, I cried after each one, I was so emotional." Melva also found the New Jersey Senior Championship games especially exciting. One year in Lincroft, N.J., when Melva was 58, she proudly medaled in the 100 meter, 200 meter, 400 meter, 800 meter, and 1500 meter races on the first day, and the 5K road race the next day. For her achievements that year she received the Governor's Council Certificate for Physical Fitness and Sports. And that same year at the Ridgewood Run, a large and well established northern New Jersey event, Melva ran all three races—the 10K, 5K, and the mile—the same day and placed first in her age group in each competition.

One of the most unique occasions in Melva's road racing career was the run with the Olympic torch. As she remembers it:

> The torch went through every state on the way to Atlanta for the Olympics of 1996, and this Garden State (New Jersey) Torch Run started in Clifton and went to Nutley. So in this small group of runners, I got to run with the torch for a quarter of a mile, and then I passed it to someone else. Now when you have the torch, everyone has to run behind you because you're leading. . . . It was a great experience, and I received a certificate for carrying the torch.

It's the Camaraderie

Whether training or racing, Melva has always preferred to be with people. When she was 52 and working at Cyanamid, she started seriously training for her races. She had four or five friends from work whom she regularly ran with from 6:00 a.m. to 7:00 a.m., and she ran with Vince, her marathon training partner, on Sundays for years from April to November. Referring to the New York City Marathons, Melva said, "The races were wonderful because I would have the Cyanamid runners come back to my house for post-marathon parties. The camaraderie was wonderful, and the best part of it was the friendship." To expand her social contacts in the sport, Melva became affiliated with several running clubs over the years, including the Cyanamid club at work, North Jersey Masters, NYRR, and currently the Morris County Striders, among others.

Melva is also a part of an 80s women's running team, the only one in the state of New Jersey, and she treasures her companionship with the other members. On the weekends they meet at the races and often go out to breakfast afterwards. During the week they call each other, confer on the race results and standings, and consider where to attend the next event. At the award ceremonies Melva appreciates the recognition, but the accolades were never the primary draw, as she explains: "But of course with all the trophies and plaques, I think the friendships mean the most, the runners themselves. The camaraderie and the running friendships, those are the real trophies, those are your real rewards."

Perseverance Personified

Melva has been blessed with good health and few injuries during her running career. In recent years, however, her hips have hampered her running and racing, and the doctors recommended hip replacement surgery. But that hasn't stopped Melva. Her right hip was surgically replaced in August of 2014, and after four months of rehab and recovery, she was back in the game. Melva ran her first race, post-surgery, The Resolution Run 5K in Hillsborough, N.J., on January 1, 2015, and, amazingly, ran in 35 more competitions that year. Then in December of 2015, Melva had the left hip surgically replaced, and afterwards spent a month at a rehab facility, followed by more physical therapy at home. Yet, defying the odds once again, after another four months of recovery, Melva was off to the races, running in the Morris Knolls 5K in Denville, N.J., on April 16, 2016, and she has been competing in two to three races a month since then. Certainly the hip surgeries have taken a toll on Melva's speed and endurance. She now restricts her competitions to five-milers and 5Ks, and her training and racing to what she calls power walking and a little jogging. But her being out there, given her limitations, is a testament to her courage and determination.

Melva shares how much the sport of road racing has meant to her:

> I feel that running and racing is a metaphor for how I lead my life. It has given me purpose, and I can go through these milestones, good and bad. There are illnesses, you have to sell your house, and

your car breaks down, and all those things. But if you have running, that's your pinnacle, and if you stay focused on it, you won't let these other things clutter up your life, and you can put these things aside. And it's given me an interest, and I will never stop being interested in other runners because they are my friends now. It's an extended family.

Keys to Melva's Success, Health, and Longevity

This was Melva's essential key:

I want to live to be 100, and I'm going to make it only by commitment to my good health, and my fitness, and my continuing to exercise, and being out there in my community of runners. . . . Even if you put only one foot outside the door, you have to have that will to do it. You have to know how important it is, and as I said, if you don't want to do it, do it anyway. My daughter and I do walks. And no matter what you're doing, if you're walking, if you're jogging or running, you're moving, and that's the most important thing, to be moving, to be active, you must be active.

Another significant factor for Melva is diet:

When I raised my children we never had Coke or Pepsi in the house. We always had fresh vegetables. . . . We don't buy anything in a box, or cholesterol-laden pastries, because I see older people that have heart attacks. They've got pacemakers, they've got defibrillators, they've got stents, and I know I don't want to go there. And the only way you can do that is prevention. You have to be your own advocate for your own good health. So what I do is think when I shop, because if there is celery and tomatoes and lettuce in the refrigerator and you're looking for something to eat, what are you going to find? You're going to find the good things. But don't bring any of that other stuff in the house, it's the worst you can do for yourself. Diet is totally important. Every day you have to think about food and what you are putting into your body.

Melva mentions self-confidence and staying positive as crucial components and states, "You have to think like Mohamed Ali. You know, he thought he was the greatest because he had that inside him. And he did accomplish a lot. So if you think you can do it, you can. If you think you can't, you can't. You have to have the power of positive thinking." Melva had one more thought to share: "The key is love. You have to love what you do and do what you love."

I had the pleasure to catch up with Melva at the very hilly and challenging New Jersey Cross Country Championship 8K in October of 2016, where she was looking in tip-top form. Yet, Melva was nudged out of first place in her age group by her 80s teammate, Shirley Pettijohn.

By the way, if you're driving through New Jersey and you happen to see the license plate, LOV2RUN, honk and wave to Melva.

Joe LaBruno, 85

Masters Winner of All Major NYRR Half Marathons at 75

W<small>HEN</small> I <small>FIRST MET</small> J<small>OE</small> at a 5K race in New Jersey in 2014, he told me this story about how he had been out on a training run of eight-to-nine miles several years ago. The driver of a car in back of him began honking his horn to get him to move off the road and wouldn't stop. Joe went right up to the car, stuck his head in the window, and said to the guy in an angry tone, "Step out of the car." Then Joe said to me, "Sure was a good thing he just drove off. He was a lot younger than me." But the incident says something about Joe's toughness and the fact that no one was going to deter him from his passion of running. Later on in our future meetings at races, I learned how well-known and beloved he is in the running community.

A highlight of Joe's running career took place at age 75 when he won all five of the borough races in the New York Road Runners (NYRR) Half Marathon Gran Prix Series in 2007 in his age group. He was victorious in the Manhattan Half Marathon in January, the Bronx Half in February, the Brooklyn Half in April, the Queens Half in September, and the Staten Island Half in October, all in the same year. Joe has all five of these half-marathon, first-place plaques tastefully displayed within one large, framed piece. Besides these accolades, he has also received the renowned NYRR Runner of the Year award

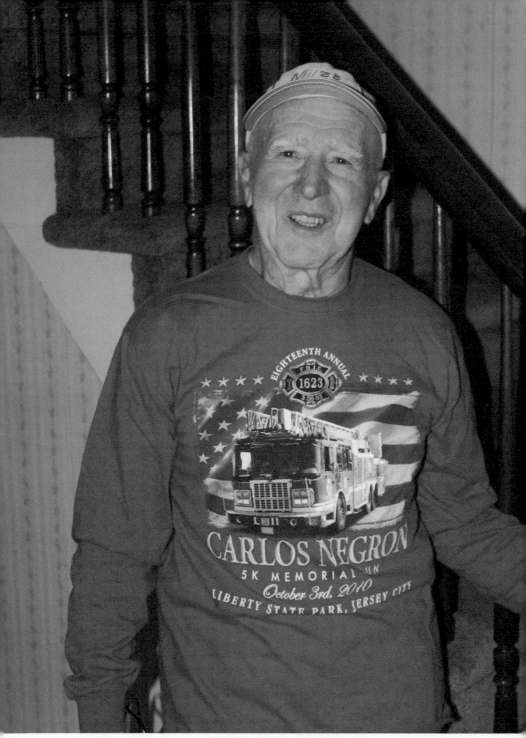

Joe Labruno, 2015

for the 80-to-84 age group. He was 80 at the time. Joe is a little like wine, getting better with age.

Joe LaBruno was born on September 2, 1931, in Bayonne, N.J., where he has resided all his life. He worked as a tool and die maker, manufacturing machinery for 36 years before retiring at 64. He has been married to Betty for 60 years, and they have eight children and 14 grandchildren.

At 57, Joe got off to a rather late start at running. He wasn't sleeping well and he thought running might help, so one day he decided to run to the store to get the newspaper. Joe commented, "I ran and it was two blocks to the store, and I thought I was going to die when I got there. And I did that for about two or three weeks, and then the store closed. So now I had to run four blocks to the store." Within a couple of months, Joe was running a mile or two at a time. But with the onset of winter Joe got discouraged:

> Then it got to be cold, and I'm out there, and it's into December, and I said to myself, "This is crazy, I'm going to quit this the end of the year." But I have eight kids, and at the end of the year at Christmas I got all these gifts—like gloves, shoes, pants. They all gave me running gear. Now I couldn't quit.

Joe Survives His First Race

Joe didn't quit, and within two years he began to compete. Yet, his first race, a four-miler, was foreboding and surreal:

> I remember that day like it was yesterday. I went to the race, and it was a hot, humid day, and I can remember I'm running and I'm bouncing off the cars. I was out of it, and I didn't know enough to stop. I mean I was so out of it that I couldn't remember anything for the last half mile. I didn't even know I finished the race. . . . I'm coming to the finish, and this police officer is directing me through the shoot, and the last thing I remember is when they pulled the oxygen mask off my face and said, "How do you feel?" My mind was blank, and I didn't know where I was. They wanted to take me to the hospital, but I refused. I didn't even know where my car was,

71

so my brother had to drive me home. I was in no shape to drive anyway. At home I had a quart and a half of orange juice, and this was like 12 o'clock noon, and I fell asleep. . . . I didn't wake up until a quarter of five. I woke up because I smelled this Italian sauce. We were having spaghetti and meatballs. I go in the kitchen and flex my muscles and tell my wife I'm ready for the next race. Oh, she wouldn't hear anything of it.

Joe thinks the heat and humidity caused him to become disoriented. The very next week Joe was off to his next race, a six-miler. This time it was a cool, rainy day, and he had no trouble.

Around this time Joe was running three miles, four to five days a week, and within a few years he had built up to 25 to 35 miles a week. His best mile was in 5:41 at age 63, a 5K in 6:47/mile at age 62, and a 10K in 7:17/mile at age 63. These were indicators of Joe's elite status in the 60s age group. He believes he has averaged about 40 races a year, and has run more than 1000 races the past quarter century. Even last year, at age 84, Joe competed in close to 30 events. The combination of the competition and the camaraderie has drawn Joe to the races. He says, "We're usually the last ones to leave, walking around talking to different people." And Joe enjoys attending the monthly meetings and picnics of the Central Jersey Road Runners.

Then the Unthinkable Happened

I was attending the New Jersey 8K Cross-Country Championships in October of 2016 to photograph some of the runners featured in this book. In the distance, not far from the finish line, I could make out an ambulance with its lights flickering, and wondered what the problem was. It turned out that Joe had fallen twice while running down a steep hill full of gravel, and the ambulance was called to pick him up. Yet he refused to go to the hospital and drove himself home. I called Joe a couple of weeks later and he assured me that he was fine and was back running and racing.

On Thanksgiving Day, after running in a 5K race, Joe didn't feel like himself. He refused again to go to the hospital, but this time his son insisted. Joe was found to have a torn aorta, the largest of the arteries that carries blood from the heart, and was in need of immediate surgery. During the procedure at the Jersey City Medical Center, Joe had a massive heart attack on the table, and the medical team had to fight to save his life. While still in the hospital, a week or so later, he finally had the surgery to repair the aorta. After two to three weeks at the Jersey City Medical Center, Joe was transferred to the Kessler Rehabilitation Center, where he remained for about 10 days.

Around New Year's, Joe returned home and continued his physical therapy. Initially, he was not allowed to go out on walks by himself, so he went with his wife or kids and built up his endurance and confidence over time. Then on May 2, 2017, Joe called to inform me he was back to racing. He had competed in the Cherry Blossom 10K in Newark, N.J., on April 9th, and the Earth Day 5K in Jersey City, N.J., on April 22nd, and was alternating jogging and walking. Joe, you are one tough dude.

Keys to Joe's Success, Health, and Longevity

Joe puts it simply: "The key is to keep on moving. You've got to keep exerting yourself." Regarding his diet, he thinks that cutting back on his food portions has helped. He also states, "I like a lot of garlic, onions, and scallions, and I have my salad every day." He adds that getting proper sleep is important and notes, "I get a lot of rest, and take a nap, and get to bed early at night."

Joe shares a few words of inevitability: "But no matter how much running you do and how much moving you do, when you start getting up in the 80s, you are slowing down."

Don Osborne at the 5K Docs Race, 2016. His bib number reflects his age.

Don Osborne, 95
At 94 He Was Still Racing

IT WAS OCTOBER 18, 2015, at the Autumn on the Sound 5K in West Haven, Conn., and in the distance I could see an older gentleman jogging toward the finish line, his jacket open and flapping on this cool, fall day. "That's my husband coming in now," exclaimed Marilyn, who was standing beside me, and she immediately got out her camera and started taking pictures. We went over to greet Don, and Marilyn introduced me to this living legend. Walking along, he quipped, "I guess all the older runners have gone inside," intimating that it was too cold for them to be outside. Don was two weeks short of his 94th birthday and still racing. At the award ceremony he received his trophy for placing in the 90+ age group, but surprisingly he had not come in first. The first place trophy was awarded to Herman Bershtein, who had recently turned 90, so Don had to settle for second place. Joe Riccio, the race director, who at 82 still races, makes it a point to have five-year age groups up to 90+ in many of his races to give older runners a fair chance of placing and winning awards.

Don Osborne was born on Halloween day, October 31, 1921, in Medway, Mass. He was the ninth of 14 children, and with eight boys the joke in the family was that they could have their own baseball team if their father was included. Being born on Halloween, however, was not advantageous. With 13 siblings focusing on their costumes and trick-or-treating, Don sadly admitted he had never had a birthday party.

In middle school Don was a bit devious, hiding the fact that he smoked from his parents. As he looked back, "I'd go fishing with my friend Brooksey, and he'd bring a supply of cigarettes and sometimes even a few cigars." One time Don got very sick to his stomach from smoking a bunch of cigars and was two hours late getting home. His mother was furious and told him to go to his room without supper. Being grateful, Don said, "Eating was last thing I wanted to do. I got under the covers and had a good night's sleep."

Three Running Mentors

Don began running on the cross-country team in high school and had to give up smoking. He said, "The coach was rather strict. He didn't want any smokers on his team, and that's when I decided I'd quit smoking." For inspiration, Don followed the career of a renowned runner:

> I became a fan of Glen Cunningham, the great miler, so he was sort of my first idol, I would say. Back in the 1930s he was the world champion miler. When he was a young boy, he was badly burned in a fire—his legs, especially. The doctors told him he would never walk again. But he overcame it all, and turned out to be the world's most famous runner at the time, and he set the world record.

Don's best mile came in the Needham High School Interscholastic Track Meet involving 13 to 14 schools where he placed 5th in a time of 4:57.6.

In 1942, Don enrolled in Gordon College of Theology in Boston as a divinity student, and it was there that he met another one of his running mentors, the great Gilbert Dodds. The two of them struck up a close friendship and ran together at the college about three days a week. Don has fond memories of the time that Gil was living with him in the winters of 1947 and 1948, and one particular memory stands out. In January of 1948, Don and Gil went down to Madison Square Garden in New York City, where Gil was to run the mile in the Milrose Games. Just before the race, Gil handed Don his personal stopwatch just to keep track of the unofficial time. At the end of the race, according to Gil's watch, it appeared to Don that his friend had set the record. Well, sure enough, Gil Dodds had, indeed, broken the world indoor record, winning the Wanamaker Mile in 4:05.3.

Training with his friend Gil helped Don prepare for his first long-distance race, the Boston Marathon of 1944, which he completed in a time of 3:15, finishing 19th out of about 150 runners. Don ran Boston again in 1947, but the results of that race and others were burned in a fire. Fortunately, Don's brother, Al, had been in attendance and had timed Don in the race in 3:20.

Clarence DeMar, a seven-time winner of the Boston Marathon, was another of Don's inspirational figures. As a kid, Don had followed his career and would go to the Boston Marathons to see him. Coincidentally, Clarence had been Don's mother's Sunday-school teacher, a fact that was never lost on Don. Then in the late 1940s, Don had the opportunity to meet this celebrity. He describes their encounter:

> I ran a race out in West Roxbury, Mass. The race was held at the site of a Catholic church, and Clarence DeMar was running in that race too. When I got a chance, I introduced myself to him and told him that my mother had always told me that he was her Sunday-school teacher. He must have been pretty young himself at that time. . . . Anyway, after I met him, it was getting close to the time for the race to begin, so he said, "Well Don, I'm glad to have met you. But, you know, before I run in a race I always get myself alone somewhere and pray. Would you like to join me?" He invited me to pray with him because I'd told him I was a theological student at Gordon. So we went away from the roadway and out in the field beside several big boulders, and so there the two of us knelt down together and prayed quietly before the race. I was impressed with him that he always prayed before running in a race.

No Running for 27 Years and Then. . .

Beginning in 1950, and for the next quarter century, Don centered his life on work and family and gave up running. Moving from Boston to Vermont after college, he began his profession as a pastor, got married, and had two daughters and two sons. Don, as a minister, performed the marriage ceremony for his current wife, Marilyn, and her first husband back in 1955. Then in 1968, Don left the ministry to teach middle school for the next 15 years. While living in Maine during his mid-50s, he tried to get his youngest son, Tom, interested in running, but it was a futile effort. Then this happened:

> One day I read in the newspaper that they were going to have a six-mile road race in Searsport. I had tried to get Tom interested in going out for cross-country in high school and running, but he'd just laughed at me. Then I said to Tom, "There is this road race they're going to have. There is a six-mile race, and for young and inexperienced runners there is a race of about a mile and a half, a downhill event all the way to the high school." So I said to Tom, "If you do the little race, I'll do the big one," and I hadn't been running for 27 years. So after he got through laughing at me, he called my bluff . . . And so the very night before the race, I went out early that evening to jog over the course. And about midway in the course there were humps of grass and a swampy area, so I had to kind of jump from hump to hump of grass just to keep my feet dry. But my one foot slipped off the top and went into the mud, and I sprained my ankle. I ran the race the next day with my ankle heavily taped up, and it was a good two months before I could walk normally after that. But I did the race. I finished in last place except for a high-school girl who finished behind me. So Tom ran the little one, and he got a prize in his event. . . . So after my ankle healed, I decided to keep jogging, and this is what started me running. And of course by that time road racing was becoming a popular sport, so I could quite easily find races.

Beginning in his mid-50s, Don had a second calling in his running career. After a hiatus of 27 years, he was back in the race, quite literally. Don calculates he has competed in about 450 races over the last four decades. And he still had the speed. In his early 60s he was running his 5Ks around 19:00, just over a 6:00/mile pace. But time intrudes, and by 87, Don was diagnosed with prostate cancer requiring surgery, and at 89 with a heart condition demanding aortic valve replacement and double by-pass surgery. This inevitably has slowed Don down, and since the heart surgery he has been limited to about five races year. For training, Don now walks a mile a day, which corresponds to six loops of his driveway, and in his races he walks and jogs a little.

The Chilly Chili 5K at 94

The Chilly Chili 5K race in Orange, Conn., is an annual event that takes place on New Year's Day and is known for its chilly weather and its hot and delicious chili. The race director, Joe Riccio, treats the 90-year-old runners to dinner on New Year's Eve and puts them up, along with their spouses, in the Marriott Hotel overnight. At 94 years of age, Don certainly qualified for the frills, but living close to the race location, he declined the invitation. The Chilly Chili of 2016 may, in fact, have been the final race of Don's running career, and at the awards ceremony he once again had to play second fiddle to Herman Bershtein, who at 90 came in first in the 90+ age group. Yet, for Don, just being in a race at his age was a miraculous feat.

Keys to Don's Success, Health, and Longevity

For Don, keeping active is essential. He states, "Continuing physical activity as long as possible, I think that's a big part of it. As long as I'm able to stand on my feet, I want to be able to walk on my legs and keep moving." Having an incentive like a race was also mentioned as a key. Don points out, "If I didn't have a goal like a race, why should I train for it? What would be the sense in going out and trying to run at all?" Furthermore, Don shared this as a reason: "I love life and I think I have an optimistic viewpoint toward the future."

In closing, Don said, "I hope you get your book published while I'm still alive." Don, I want you to know, I'm furiously working to make this happen.

Nat Finestone, 2015

Nat Finestone, 87
A Runner Comes of Age

ONE MORNING IN OTTAWA, CANADA, Nat was out delivering news-papers on his daily route in the bitter cold and he could no longer feel his feet. Later on that day something went terribly wrong, as Nat reveals to us:

> When I was a teenager, I came home to die. . . . I could not straighten my legs. So I went to the hospital, and they diagnosed me with chronic nephritis, which is a kidney disease. I weighed 200 pounds, and there was water all through my body. I could put my finger in my head and there were deep gullies where the water was. My parents were told I was not going to recover and, if I did, I wouldn't live through my 20s. And my mother had a doctor that she used to get me out of the hospital, and he let her have control of my condition. My mother was not well educated, but I believe that God used her to save my life. She went on the theory, if you give the body a chance, it'll heal itself. So she put me on a strict fast, and I was only taking in fluids for at least a month. We had people come and pray for me. And one day I soaked the entire bed, and every-thing left me all at once. Well, I was out of school for an entire year.

Nat Finestone was born on March 19, 1929, in Ottawa. At 16 he made a full and miraculous recovery from the illness described above. After graduating from Rutgers University, Nat moved to Philadelphia and took a job with a large supermarket company as

81

an analyst. After five years he received a promotion, returned to New Jersey to finish his career, and took early retirement at 55. He tied the knot with his wife, Carol, when he was 39, and they have been happily married for 48 years.

From childhood through his 50s, besides some intermittent bike riding, Nat was not very active. But at 60 that was about to change. Nat says, "I was having problems with elimination, with having a bowel movement, and I thought running would help me in that regard, and it did. And I was getting older and I thought being more active would be good for me." For the next 13 years, Nat was off and running three miles every day. Then, at age 73, he went to see his doctor, who said, "If you're running every day, why not enter some races?" Nat says that at the time, he didn't even know there were races, but he quickly discovered them—and his love for competition. He ran about 10 races a year, mostly 5Ks, until he was close to 80, and since then has been averaging 30 races a year, including some longer events from the 10K to the half marathon. With the encouragement of a fellow competitor, Joe LaBruno, Nat joined the Central New Jersey Road Runners at age 78. He believes that the club has been a major inspiration for improving his running performance. For his age, these times are exceptional: At 77, he ran a 5K in 27:40 at 8:54/mile, and at age 79, he ran a 10K in 59:02 at 9:30/mile. And here's one sure to impress: At age 83, Nat ran the Super Hero Half Marathon in 2:19, at 10:35/mile. A salute to you, Nat.

In recent years, Nat has taken a few falls due to fallen tree branches on his early morning runs, but he refuses to forgo these fleet-footed jogs before the sun rises. Here's why: "I steal glances at the sky. When you see Orion and you see the Big Dipper and the moon, when you see the sunrise in the East and the moon setting in the West, I enjoy that. And when it gets a little lighter, I enjoy the beauty of the dawn."

Keys to Nat's Success, Health, and Longevity

"You cannot understand me without understanding my faith," says Nat. "I believe the body is the temple of the Holy Spirit. We are not to abuse our body, and God desires me to take care of myself." He also remembers, "I came so near to death when I was a teenager that I realized my mortality. And I would say that has also been an inspiration for me to pay attention to my well-being."

Some insight from Nat: "Life is like a race, and running a good race involves a lot of factors. Your attention to what you believe, and to what you eat, and to how you conduct yourself as a human being, will enable you to have a good performance."

Patricia O'Hanlon with 50 States Marathon Certificate. Photo taken in 2016.

Patricia O'Hanlon, 73
Ran a Marathon in Every State

Getting to the start of the Las Vegas Marathon was no easy task, as Patricia recalls:

The start was at one end of the strip, and I was staying at the other end at my hotel. I'd scoped it all out the day before, and figured the morning of the race, I would drive close to the start, which I thought was only a couple of miles away. But it turned out to be longer, maybe about three and a half miles. Anyway, the morning of the race, I get in my car with the stuff I take to a race, and come out of the garage, and there are all these roadblocks all over the place. They had closed the roads already, and this was a good hour before the race started. So I see a police officer there, you know, telling everybody, "No, no, no!" And I said, "Well, I have to get down there. How can I get there this morning?" And he says, "I can't tell you that ma'am." If you could have viewed this site from a helicopter it would have looked like a Key Stone Cops comedy, because everybody was making U-turns and trying to find a way out of there. I said, "Well, I'm not wasting anymore time." I put the car back in the garage, put my pack on my back, and started trotting down to the start, which I didn't think was as far as it was. And as I'm almost at the start line, the lead runner is coming at me. I says, "Well, I'm here, I'm doing this race, I don't care." I got to the start, which was in the process of being taken apart. So I go up to this fellow and he says, "You're not the only one late, we just took care of somebody else. Get yourself ready, give me your bag, whatever you want to leave behind, and I'll have it for you at the finish." And I said, "Goodbye bag, I'll never see you again. . . ." Well, I didn't plan on going back to Nevada, you know. So I was there, I'm going to do this race.

Although she had to run to the start line and had gotten there a half hour late, Patricia still placed third in her late-60s age group. And not only that, she retrieved her bag at the finish line, right where she was told it would be. Adversity had been met head-on, and for Patricia the marathon in Nevada was in the books.

Patricia O'Hanlon was born on June, 16, 1943, in Brooklyn, N.Y. Influenced by her parents to attend secretarial school for practical reasons, Patricia took her first job as an administrative assistant with Youngstown Sheet and Tube Company, remaining there for 10 years. After the business relocated, she secured a position with Brooklyn Union Gas Company for the next 27 years, beginning as a secretary and eventually moving up to executive assistant to the chairman of the board and finishing her career there. She married Frank in 1965, but the relationship was not satisfying and ended in divorced after 21 years.

While still living and working in Brooklyn, Patricia became inspired to try running after gaining about 25 pounds. She recollects the following:

> In my 40s I realized I had packed on a few extra pounds and decided I wanted to get rid of them. So first I tried every diet, you know, and soon got sick of every single one of them. Then I knew I had to do something physical. So I went out to do a little run, and I couldn't even go around the block. Much to my surprise, I got winded.

To build up some endurance, Patricia took an aerobics class at a local gym, and within a month she was running the entire three-mile loop around a cemetery near her home. Then, soon after joining the

Prospect Park Track Club, she entered her first race with a couple of friends in Staten Island. After the 5K race she remembers, "We were sitting around waiting, and I heard my name called. I had placed in the first race I ever ran in! So that kind of got me hooked."

A couple of years after she started running, Patricia decided to do her first marathon. She was 50 and she chose the most prestigious one of all, the New York City Marathon, which she completed in a respectable 4:17. "I only did one marathon a year and it was New York for five years in a row," she says. "Then one year I didn't get in, and I said to heck with New York, I'm going to take my running shoes someplace else." In 1998, Patricia ran the Philadelphia Marathon at age 55, and she ran four more marathons the next year, including the Virginia Beach Marathon in a personal best time of 3:47, the Boston Marathon a month later, and the Hartford and Rhode Island Marathons in the fall.

The seed was planted and the number of marathons were mushrooming, as Patricia notes:

> After I got a few of these different states down, a friend who was almost done doing the 50 states says to me, "Oh, you have a nice base there, why don't you do all 50?" So, I humored him and said, "Oh, yah, sure, okay," but I never, never, thought I'd do it. But then, low and behold, before I knew it, I was at the halfway point. And I said, you know what, I have to step things up because I'm not a spring chicken anymore. So if I want to do this in my lifetime, I have to do them closer together.

But the Tucson, Arizona marathon, in particular, presented Patricia with a hardship she would not soon forget, one that could have dissuaded her from pursuing her 50-state goal. She describes the unfortunate circumstances:

> I've gone to a lot of races by myself, but this one I happened to travel to with the friend who provoked me into doing all of this—Francisco Rodrigues. He's done a marathon in every state twice. So I arrive in Arizona, and I'm really sick, and the next day I spent most of the morning in the bathroom. But I said, you know, I'm here, I've got to

do this. Even if I have to walk, I'm going to do it. So I did, and I made 13 unscheduled pit stops, without port-o-johns and without bushes. You know, Arizona doesn't have bushes. I had a stomach virus and it was horrible, the worst thing. But anyway, I would run, you know, and whenever I needed to, I'd go off in a ditch somewhere and do what I had to do. So I continued on my way, stopping and running, stopping and running, and I had a terrible time.

Her friend, Francisco, who knew Patricia had been sick, was keeping track of her on the marathon course with his phone app and knew she was slow but not stuck in a hospital somewhere. Patricia was grateful to have her friend meet her at the finish line. Somehow she was able to put this experience behind her and move along in her marathon quest.

Yet time wasn't on her side. Patricia was 63 in 2007, and still 17 state marathons short of her goal. However, her legs were strong, and she cranked out eight more marathons in 2008, and another nine in 2009, as she traveled from state to state all over the country. Finally, Patricia completed her 50th state, and after all marathon results were authenticated, she was awarded a large certificate symbolizing her awesome feat, which she had attractively framed. It reads as follows:

The 50 States Marathon Club recognizes and honors Patricia O'Hanlon, Jersey City, N.J., for outstanding athletic accomplishment and achievement of finishing a full marathon of 26.2 miles in all 50 states of the United States of America. Finisher of the 50 states at the Asbury Park Relay Marathon in Asbury Park, N.J., on Oct. 18, 2009. (Patricia had run as a relay team of one in this, her final marathon.)

Patricia met her goal of running a marathon in every state. But here's the amazing part. She completed half of those marathons in her 60s, and that's a stunning achievement in and of itself. Furthermore, Patricia believes she is the first woman from the state of New Jersey to have completed a marathon in all 50 states. And to top it off, she placed in 39 of her 50 state marathons, winning her age group in many of them. Altogether, Patricia has run 56 marathons.

For the past quarter century Patricia has run the 5K to the marathon, averaging about 40 races a year, and estimates having competed in over 1000 races in her running career. There were years when she averaged as many as 70 races a year, while occasionally running two or three races on a weekend end and one on a weekday. For training, she would run after work from 7:00 p.m. to 8:00 p.m., six days a week. Presently, she has cut back to about 25 races a year and has curtailed her running to three days a week. For cross-training purposes, Patricia bikes once a week, goes to a boxing gym (mostly for footwork and flexibility), jumps rope, uses free weights, and takes a yoga class.

Running Marathons as a Cancer Survivor

In her late 50s, long before she had finished her 50th state marathon, Patricia was diagnosed with breast cancer and had major surgery and reconstruction. After this fight for survival, Patricia remained resolute and continued her march toward her marathon goal. However, completing over 25 marathons in her 60s as a cancer survivor was no small undertaking, and a testament to her courage and fortitude.

Patricia has sustained two major running injuries. The first happened on a 90-mile race called the River to Sea Relay in New Jersey, when she was about 60. She had twisted her ankle on some gravel before the race, but proceeded to run her two sections of two and six miles. She says, "The last segment ended at a beach and I ran right into the water. When I took off my shoe and sock I didn't recognize my own foot. It was the color of the rainbow and was blown up like a football." As it turned out, Patricia had run her eight miles on a fractured ankle, and it took her six weeks of recovery in a cast before she was able to return to running.

A second major injury occurred during a 10K race, when Patricia was 66. She recalled, "I started running from here maybe to the door. I didn't feel a thing, and the next thing I knew I was on the ground and an EMT was on my chest. I had what they call a spontaneous brain bleed." Patricia was taken to the hospital and found she couldn't move her right leg from the knee down. She spent a week in the hospital and another two weeks at a rehab center receiving physical therapy. Patricia credits the running community with lifting her spirits and assisting in her recovery. She had many friends from a variety of running clubs who visited her in the hospital and rehab center and sent cards. Fortunately, besides a slight problem with her right foot, Patricia has made a full recovery and is back to running on the roads and competing in the races.

Keys to Patricia's Success, Health, and Longevity

Support from the running community and the sociability it has offered, Patricia believes, are major contributors to her success and longevity in the sport of road racing. She meets and has breakfast regularly with a group of runners, the majority of whom have also run marathons in all 50 states, and frequently after races, she will go out with fellow racers for refreshments.

Patricia also shared this anecdote:

> When I went to visit the Intrepid some time ago, I found out that it was launched into service in 1943, which is the year I was born. Well, the name of the ship is the Intrepid, and I thought, you know, that's a good word for me, intrepid. . . . Don't give up, just keep on going. Like the old Timex commercial, "Takes a licking and keeps on ticking."

At the end of the interview Patricia had some parting words: "When it comes my time to leave this world, I'm not going to be pretty, but my goal is still to be fit."

Bob Davidson, 87

Author of the Book
"All Runners Are Crazy"

BY HIS 60s, Bob was a fast and talented age-group runner, but when he first started out racing in his 50s, he had not yet mastered the nuances and subtleties of the sport. For example, Bob nearly lost his teeth in this 5K race he describes below. No, he didn't fall, but let Bob tell you what happened:

> I think it was the Early Bird Race in West Hartford, Conn., and I was probably in my late 50s. . . . And there was one fellow that I was very competitive with, and he was probably the best runner in our age group in this immediate area, so I wanted to do well. And to lose any time unnecessarily, of course, would defeat my purpose. It was a two-loop race—a 10K. And when I ran almost the first loop, almost to the starting line again, I realized that because of a new bridge that covers the upper part of my mouth, I was breathing so hard that the bridge was getting loose. And I thought, "Boy, if I choke on this thing, it's going to kill me." So I've got to get rid of it, but what do I do with it? I figured, well, I'm going by where my wife would be standing where the race started. So I took out the bridge, wrapped it in my hat, and threw it to her and said, "Don't lose the hat."

That's thinking on your feet. Bob got his bridge back and all was well.

Bob Davidson, 2015

Bob Davidson was born on July 1, 1929, in Worcester, Mass. In high school he played football for three years. He states, "If you can imagine a skinny 145-pound right tackle . . . I wasn't good. We had a small school, and they were desperate for players. Really, we had 48 people in our graduating class. So if the coach saw someone who could walk fast and didn't fall down, you were on the team." But besides playing football Bob began running at this time, and he and a few of his buddies formed their own unofficial team. He proudly proclaims, "I was captain of an undefeated track team," but admits that the team never ran in any authorized races.

For the next 35 years, Bob focused on working and on raising a family. He married his high-school sweetheart, Janice, when he was 21, and they had two daughters, Deb and Sue, and a son, Cole. By his mid-50s, with his children grown and on their own, Bob recognized that three decades of office work for an insurance company was not contributing to his health or happiness and recalls, "When they gave me an opportunity to escape at 55, I jumped on that." With early retirement Bob re-invented himself. He went into his own wood-working and furniture repair business for the next six years and focused on his physical well-being. He says, "I started to jog for health reasons. I was overweight and had high blood pressure." With the time flexibility to run and train, Bob soon took up the sport of road racing and became a serious runner. In the process he lost 25 pounds, got his blood pressure back within the normal range, and lowered his pulse rate from 80 to about 55. He adds, "My self-esteem improved along the way too."

Running and racing gave Bob a new sense of self. He confesses:

I never was satisfied that I was really good at anything. That's how I felt about myself. Fortunately, I had friends and relatives who had a higher opinion of me than I did. And then I found in running that I was good at something and that fed my depleted ego and made me pleased with myself. And now I found something I'm good at and can take some pride in. And I've gotten positive feedback. Kids who are only 15 and 16 would come up to me and say, "You're an inspiration."

Four Medals at the National Senior Games at Age 80

By the time Bob was in his 60s, his race results were eye-popping. At age 60 he ran a 10K in a 6:42/mile pace and, at 69, a 5K in 7:04/mile. Overall, Bob has averaged about 20 races a year for 30 years, and he believes he has competed in over 500 events in his running career. He also has fond memories of attending the Senior Olympic Games from age 55 to 75. These USA Track & Field national championship competitions take place every other year. But the most memorable was in his final entry of the Senior Games at Stanford University in Palo Alto, Calif., when he was 80. As Bob explains, "Thirteen members of my family were in the stands. Some of them were from Oregon, some were from Pennsylvania, and some were local from Connecticut. I had my own cheering section, and I ran four races in four days." Bob entered the 800 meters, the 1500 meters, the 5K, and the 10K, placing third and winning a medal in each event, to great fanfare from his family. But winning those four medals came with some risk, as Bob reveals to us:

> So I was carrying a lot of medals around with me for the next few days. . . . The funniest time was when we were at the hotel and everybody else was down at the pool. I had changed into my swimming trunks and I came down to the pool and they said, "Bob, this is the first time we've seen you without your medals." So I grabbed my swimming shorts and they jingled, and I went into the pool at great risk of sinking with all the medals.

Since age 54, when he began running, Bob has been blessed with reasonably good health. His only injuries have resulted from taking a fall and tearing a few ligaments in his ankle, and having arthroscopic surgery for a torn meniscus of the right knee. In the past couple of years, however, a diagnosis of COPD, Chronic Obstructive Pulmonary Disease, has slowed Bob down considerably. Then, on the anniversary of his son's tragic death two years before, Bob fell down a flight of stairs and was seriously injured. Bleeding and in shock, he somehow managed to stagger to the neighbor's house to save his own life. It took months of healing to recuperate from this traumatic incident, and the doctor was firm: No more running. Bob ran his last race at 86 in early August of 2015, and although he misses the sport terribly, he still fondly reminisces upon the three decades of his distinguished running career.

Excerpts from Bob's Book

My wife believes anyone over 4 should know better than to run as fast as they can unless it is for something especially rewarding, like being first in a department store sale. She believes ALL RUNNERS ARE CRAZY. (Thus, the title of the book)

When you are racing at age 80 or above and some child 6 years old or younger passes you early in the race . . . Their parents should tell these children it is not nice to pass anyone fifteen times their size and age.

My trainer/manager (his wife) has often commented that she is amazed that so many injury-laden, suffering, disabled, crippled runners could even get to the starting line. What really astonishes her most is that once the starter fires the beginning of the race, all these self-proclaimed zombies take off like their wives had just found the picture of their old girlfriend in their wallet.

As far as how fast you tell people you used to run—it goes like this: The older you get the faster you can say you used to run. No one old enough to know the truth can remember anyway.

Some studies indicate that genetics account for 30-50% of our aging process. That is good news. It means our actions impact our aging process 50-70%.

Keys to Bob's Success, Health, and Longevity

Emphasizing the need to keep active, Bob makes this point:

I think if you're not physically active, including some weight work and some exercise that puts a strain on your cardiovascular system, that your lung capacity is going to be diminished as you get older, and your muscle mass will get less and less if you don't do any weight training. . . . Running has been one of the keys to my longevity.

Bob also credits his wife, Janice, with helping him succeed:

I would think the support of my wife has been a major contributing factor. Because while she has gone through a lot of boring races, spent time traveling to and from various races, and sometimes spent time in restaurants with other runners that she doesn't particularly care for, all of that has made my life easier and more pleasant. And I think if I didn't get that kind of support, that I probably wouldn't have been as successful as I have been.

Janice only missed two of over 500 races that Bob competed in. They have been happily married for 66 years.

Furthermore, the sense of competition is critical for Bob. "Being competitive," he says, "that's made me successful. I don't like to lose at anything. That's not necessarily good, but that's the way I'm built." And the fellowship with runners is also a significant factor. He explains:

The friendships that I've developed over the years with other runners is important. I think I've received as much pleasure out of their accomplishments as I have of my own. I've tried to be, and I think I have been, very supportive of them. And I've encouraged them and critiqued them, as they have critiqued me.

Bob's advice to younger runners: "Enjoy yourself, train hard, don't let it interfere with your family responsibilities, and run like hell."

Sid Howard, 77

Won over 50 National and World Masters Titles

The competition in the middle of Manhattan was fierce and came down to a photo finish. Sid takes us to the race:

> It was the 5th Avenue Mile in 1999, and I'd turned 60. I started running this race in 1983, when I was 44 years old, and I'm the only runner that has run every Masters 5th Avenue Mile, and that's 33 races. . . . Before that race, on Feb. 26th, on my birthday, I broke the world record for men 60 and over in the 800 meters. This gave me the confidence, because I'd never beaten Fay Bradley. He beat me three straight times, and he's a National Masters Hall of Famer. We start off running, and he's in front of me. I was behind him the whole race, no more than about 10 meters. And when it got to 200 meters to go—they have a big sign that says 200 meters—I sped up past him, and I thought I was in the clear. And then he came back, and he passed me with maybe 75 meters to go, and then I passed him again with maybe 50 meters to go, and he came back, and we were just neck and neck and neck, and at the finish line my chest beat him at the tape. That was my first-ever win of the 5th Avenue Mile, and since then I've won ten 5th Avenue Mile races since I've turned 60.

Sid won the race in a time of 5:12.15, with Fay not far behind at 5:12.41. Just a quarter of a second separated the two runners. But that

Sid Howard, 2016

victory appeared to break a barrier for Sid, and with that win, the flood gates opened and the national and world championships started flowing.

Before long, Sid had piled up an impressive list of masters (age group) titles in his specialty events—the 800 meters, 1500 meters, and the mile. His first title win was in 1986, when he was 47 years of age, at the USA Track & Field, Indoor National Championships in Baton Rouge, La., eight years after he'd started running. He won the mile in 4:35, and was victorious in the two mile. Sid also set American masters indoor records in the 800 meters in 2004 at age 65 in 2:19.4, and in 2009 at age 70 in 2:33.4 Overall, Sid has won over 50 masters national championships, both indoor and outdoor, from 1983 to 2011.

In the WMA, World Masters Athletics, better known as the World Games, Sid captured eight masters world championships from 1983 to 2014. In the indoor championships of 2004 in Sindelfingen, Germany, at age 65, Sid won gold in both the 800 meters and 1500 meters. And he won both these events again in 2006 at age 67 in Linz, Austria, and in 2010 at age 71 in Kamloops, Canada. In the World Masters Outdoor Championships in 2009 in Lahti, Finland, at age 70, he took home the gold in the 1500 meters in 5:19. And in his final appearance in the World Games at age 75 in Budapest, Hungry, Sid took the silver medal in the 800 meters in 2:53, just a second behind the winner.

Sid Howard was born on February 26, 1939, in Elizabeth, N.J. In high school he wanted to play football, but his physique didn't measure up. Sid explains, "I went out for football, and I weighed like a hundred pounds, and the coach said, 'You could be the manager.' So my best friend said, 'Sid, let's go out for cross-country.' I never knew I was a runner. Running found me, I didn't find running." By his junior year, Sid was the top runner in his high school, but he never took his studies seriously. He states, "In 1956 when school ended, I failed—not only math, but I was the number-one clown in woodshop, and I failed that too. I made everybody laugh, but the joke was on me."

After 11th grade, Sid dropped out of high school and never returned. In the fall of that year he joined the U.S. Air Force at 17, and by 18, married his girlfriend. Sid points out, "She was 16 and pregnant, and in those days it was automatic, you get married. And that lasted for 39 years, and we had six kids." After being discharged from the air force at 21, Sid found employment the next ten years working in Manhattan on duplicating machines, but eventually, he discovered his niche by starting his own messenger service business. It proved to be profitable and a lifelong career. With the help of the GI Bill, he and his family bought a home in Plainfield, N.J., in 1972, where he still resides today. And Sid finally returned to school. From 1974 to 1991, he went to college intermittently and graduated from Kean University with a B.A. degree in social work at age 59, with his grandkids attending his graduation. With his own business thriving, however, Sid has never had to work as a social worker.

In his late 30s, Sid began running with his four sons, and as an incentive would give them each a dollar for every mile they ran. Twice a month or so, they would all go out together and do a five-mile loop near their home. Then one day Sid's life changed forever, as he recalls:

> My son came and said, "Dad, they have a race for old men at the high school." I didn't even know they had races for people out of high school. Well, I won the race, a 5:05 mile in my first race. I had trained with my neighbor for three weeks doing 400 meter intervals. I remembered what I used to do in high school, and it was muscle memory that came back. But when I found out they had other races, I went crazy, and I was going everywhere to run. It was like I was born again. And three months later in October, I ran my first New York City Marathon.

At 39, after running for only four months, Sid ran the New York City Marathon in a dazzling 3:02. Just one month later he ran the New Jersey Marathon in 3:03. Sid jumped right in, even though he admits to not knowing quite what he was doing. The morning before that first New York City Marathon he hadn't eaten because he thought the lighter he was the better. But after hitting the wall with no fuel left in his tank, he had to walk and jog at the end of the race. After a time, however, Sid caught on to the nuances of the sport and became an elite masters runner, as some of Sid's personal best times attest. For instance, he ran a 5K in 16:20, at 5:16/mile, in the New Jersey Masters Championships at age 45; the Harlem 10K in 33:27, at 5:24/mile at age 46; a half marathon at the Hispanic Games in Central Park in 1:14, at 6:00/mile at age 45; and the New York City Marathon in 2:46, at 6:22/mile at age 42.

Ten-Time Winner of the NYRR Runner of the Year Award

In the 38 years Sid has been running, he has averaged about 30 races a year, totaling close to 1100 races. And although his expertise has always been on the track in the shorter events, like the 800 meters, 1500 meters, and the mile, Sid continued to run the more traditional, long-distance races into his 60s and 70s. His ability and success were acknowledged when he won the acclaimed New York Road Runners (NYRR) Runner of the Year award for his age group 10 times, the last prize bestowed in 2010 at age 70.

For the most part, Sid has been able to avoid major injuries. Yet, a lingering hamstring problem, which began 20 years ago, has needed attention, and Sid found just the right treatment. He describes it as follows: "I learned how to take these ice-baths, which helped me. I'd get a bag of ice and throw it in the tub and sit in there for 12 to 15 minutes. The first three minutes I'd shiver, and after that you're numb. And it helps speed the recovery and rid the inflammation."

Unfortunately, Sid aggravated his hamstring injury after running a half marathon in Bermuda in 2014, and since then has essentially given up his training and racing. He still jogs two to three miles a few times a week, and will run up to eight miles at an easy pace with a charity group he coaches for the New York City Marathon about once a week. Sid is also the varsity track-and-field coach for an all-girls high school in Manhattan and works with the NYRR club to instruct seniors in exercising and stretching.

The sport of running has been very rewarding to Sid:

It has given me a sense of purpose and has changed my whole life. I didn't have anything that was of importance to me, and it made my life very important. It gave me the opportunity to travel and meet people from all over the world. I am known as an ambassador of the sport, and I have run on five continents. And seeing these people older than you, 80-year-old women jumping over hurdles. . . . All of these things are so inspiring.

Keys to Sid's Success, Health, and Longevity

A key element of health for Sid is diet:

I became a vegetarian a couple of months before I started running in February of 1978. . . . The food that I'm putting in my body is going to give me better success for running as well as for recovering. In the morning I have almonds, pecans, and walnuts, a handful of raisons, a spoonful of chia seeds, then raw oatmeal on top, and a half banana, strawberries, blueberries, blackberries, and almond milk. That lasts me six hours and I only eat two meals a day. My second main meal would be any type of a salad and grains. It may be a combination of beans, rice potatoes, or quinoa. But throughout the day I'm snacking on nuts, raisons, bananas, apples and grapes. Every night before I go to bed I have grapes.

Sid mentions the importance of training:

In order for you to be a competitive runner, you have to train. It's essential. But I dialed back my training, and I found I was more successful. I found out that more is less and less is more in training. I was lucky because I found the perfect amount of training that I needed, and I became successful with that."

Sid closed our conversation on this note:

Runners don't have common sense, John. If we had common sense, we wouldn't be doing what we do. We run in the cold, we run in the rain, we run in the snow, we run when it's hot, we run when we're angry, we run when we're happy. I love being a part of this fraternity, believe me. . . . When I'm coming around the curve, down the stretch, and then there be a coffin waiting for me and I could just jump in that coffin. They close it, and that's the way he wanted to go.

Jim Stevens, 84

At 81 Ran the
New York City Marathon

J IM GOT OFF TO A RATHER SLOW START with his running:

> I wanted to be a runner, so I joined the cross-country team at Fair-
> field Prep School. Two weeks later I caught pneumonia, and I didn't
> run again for 20 years. So 20 years later in 1967, I started again. I
> ran for a few weeks and the knee went and I stopped running. Well,
> I didn't run again for another 10 years. In 1977, I started running
> again and this time I said, "I'm going to do it right."

And Jim has never looked back. He found a group of four or five
guys who ran together every other day or so, and he was delighted
to have the company and conversation. Jim says, "I don't like to run
alone, and I can't run with others without talking. It's very social."
He also states, "I love to be in competition. I always tell Ann (his
wife), after a race it's like a cocktail party. Everybody talks to everybody, and instead of alcohol and fancy food, you have bagels and
water and everybody is happy."

Jim has been a competitive runner for nearly 40 years, and in the
past three decades has averaged 30 to 35 races a year, competing in
some 1000 events. Yet, as the interview revealed, Jim was not interested in setting any masters records or remembering his best times
for races. It was always more about staying in shape, fraternizing

Jim Stevens at the 5K Docs Race, 2016

with people, and having fun. There was one race, however, that Jim did take seriously, and that was the New York City Marathon. It was as if he had a kinship connection with this larger-than-life phenomenon: He proudly displays in his home the 22 medals that represent the number of times he has completed the marathon. He ran this race six times in his 50s, seven times in his 60s, and eight times in his 70s. But he didn't stop there. With the throngs of onlookers lining Central Park, Jim crossed the finish line in his marathon finale at the tender age of 81.

Jim Stevens was born on May 28, 1932, in Bridgeport, Conn. After graduating from Long Island Tech, he worked for a large insurance company as a life underwriter for 23 years. For the past 30 to 40 years, Jim has been property manager of his own seven apartments, doing nearly all the physical labor for the maintenance and modernization of the units. Jim has been married to his second wife, Ann, for 41 years and has three children from his first marriage.

Keys to Jim's Success, Health, and Longevity

Jim remarks, "Well, first of all, I was blessed with a healthy body. . . . My mother was born in 1900 and died in 2000, and she lived to be 100." Jim also emphasizes having a healthy lifestyle is important and points out, "50 years ago I said, 'I'm going to make my health a hobby.' My goal was to keep my weight down, my blood pressure down, and my cholesterol down. Well, I'm doing it by being active and eating what I think is right."

In 1999 Jim fell off a scaffolding and fractured his left foot. He showed me the X-ray of the broken heel bone and how the bone was reset with two, large, inch and 5/8 screws. Jim had this to say about his predicament: "It never bothered me, like it never happened. The screws were in there to keep it in place until it healed. They were never removed and never will be." It's truly a wonder how anyone can run on a foot that has two huge screws still in place. This man is full of mettle.

Betty Holroyd at the Chilly Chili 5K Run, 2016. Her bib number reflects her age.

Betty Holroyd, 90
Loves Racing with her Grandkids

Bᴇᴛᴛʏ sᴛᴀʀᴛᴇᴅ ʀᴜɴɴɪɴɢ ʟᴀᴛᴇʀ ɪɴ ʟɪғᴇ and attributes her inspiration to her two sons, Bill and Curtis. She reminisces:

> I began running when I was 56 or 57. I was sitting on the patio one sunny Sunday morning with my husband Bill reading the paper with our five children. We were sitting there enjoying our coffee, and our two boys were going out for a run and said, "Mom and Dad, come on and get off your butts, and come out with us to the Choate running track." And so Bill and I went out to the track, and I couldn't even run a quarter of the way around. I had to stop and walk—I'd never done any running. . . . So we started running, and it got us going, let's put it that way.

From that day forward, Betty and Bill were runners. They ran together on weekends, and Betty ran on her own once or twice a week after work. About five years later their daughter, Kristine, also a runner, encouraged her parents to try competing in races, and they all began going to the competitions together. With their kids and grandkids joining Betty and Bill at the races, running competitively became a family affair. They were known to have as many as 10 relatives in a race, and the Holroyd clan often won awards for having the most family members at those events. When interviewing Betty in her home, I witnessed several exquisite three-generation trophies with multiple running figures adorning each. She has found special pleasure in racing with her family, and, in recent years, with her two grandchildren, Betsy and Katie. Unfortunately, her husband, Bill, had to stop running when he was 80, about 12 years ago.

One memorable competition for Betty was a three-generation family race at Wesley Village, a senior-care community, when she was 87. Betty remembers it in this way:

> One family race that does stand out was in Shelton, Conn. It was at an assisted-living place, and many of the residents were in wheel-chairs, and they were right there as we came in cheering us on. That made me think that could be me in a wheelchair and how blessed I am to be healthy and be able to run. . . . And we all won a prize for our age group.

Betty Holroyd was born on May, 13, 1926, in Waterbury, Conn., and has always lived within 25 miles of her birthplace. Because her father changed jobs, the family moved to Wallingford when she was 10, and Betty has lived in the town ever since. She has been married to Bill for 66 years, and they have three daughters, two sons, and six grandchildren. Betty had a long and satisfying career in nursing before retiring at 72.

Although never a fast runner, Betty still won many awards and trophies, but admits that often there was no one else in her age group. Yet, on her best days in her early 80s, she was running a 5K in the 13:00/mile range. Two days after her 90th birthday, Betty ran the Sea Dog 5K in Cheshire, Conn., a momentous milestone. She now combines jogging and walking during her competitions. She has raced roughly once a month for the past quarter century, which equates to about 300 races over her running career. And with the exception of falling on icy pavement, breaking her wrist, and being in a cast for six weeks, Betty has remained miraculously free of injuries.

Keys to Betty's Success, Health, and Longevity

One of the primary keys for Betty is family support. She ran and raced regularly with her husband, her two sons and their three children, and with Kristine and her two kids. Betty points out, "The joy of being able to do the races with my grandchildren, that's what motivates me most." Betty describes herself as an optimist and remarks, "Every life has hardships, good times and bad times, and you must concentrate on the good times and be thankful." And she adds, "My faith, my belief in god, has had a lot to do with my happy life."

Advice from Betty: "Eat healthy and find something that will keep you active. Maybe it's tennis that you play three times a week. We use running but there are many other active sports. . . . If you stay healthy, you're able to enjoy so many other things when you get to be 90 years old."

David Adams, 2015

David Adams, 77
The Barefoot Runner

WHAT IS IT LIKE TO RUN BAREFOOT on the roads? Well, it isn't always pleasant, as David reveals to us. While attending a brain research conference in Gagra, Georgia, before the breakup of the Soviet Union, David went out for a run:

> And then I hear this noise. The soles of my feet had come off. This whole thing was flapping, and underneath was just very tender because it was under the skin. I had torn the skin off. That wasn't too much fun, actually. It was hurting when it was flapping. When I looked down, I said, "Hey, my feet have come off."

David's thick skin betrayed him because he had laid off running for a few months to recover from tendinitis. The thick skin had thinned and softened. Normally, running barefoot creates a leathery, thickening of the skin. David says, "When you run barefoot you have very, very thick skin. Whenever I meet carpenters, I say, 'Let me see your hand,' because my foot looks like the hand of a carpenter."

David Adams was born on May 13, 1939, in Webster Groves, Mo. He began running on the track team in high school but mentions not being very good, although his brother had been a state champion. For his undergraduate work, David went to Columbia College in New York City and would run around the campus neighborhood. Then David went on to graduate school at Yale University for a dual Ph.D. degree in psychology and physiology, and accepted a position at Wesleyan University doing research on the brain for the next 25 years while commuting from New Haven, Conn.

While working at Wesleyan, David became more earnest about his running. In his late 30s he tried competing in a couple of races, but found he was having knee problems. After running five to ten miles his knees would cramp up. It was at this time that David met the great barefoot runner, Charlie Robbins, a two-time national marathon champion, and they did some training runs together. To address the difficulty with David's knees, Charlie said, "Well, if you run barefoot you won't have a problem with that because you'll have a more stable foot plant." David took Charlie's advice and has been a barefoot runner now for nearly four decades. But when considering barefoot running, body type must be kept in mind. At 100 pounds and slight of built Charlie ran like a gazelle, while David, at 175 pounds and with a large-boned, muscular build, hit the pavement with greater impact.

Three Barefoot Stories

David illuminates some of the obstacles and pitfalls of a barefoot runner in these vignettes. "I've heard glass crunch under my feet while running," he says. "I get a piece of glass every couple of hundred miles, and I always carry a safely pin to take it out." In this first story, however, the safety pin was not sufficient:

> I remember a funny story about this guy named George Brown, who wrote the column on running for the *Hartford Currant* over the years, and George was terribly upset that I could beat him. He was a little bit older than me, and he was a pretty good runner, and he and I were pretty much the same speed. So once we ran a 5K race down at Bridgeport on the 4th of July, and it was hotter than hell. We started off warming up in the field, and I got a big piece of glass in my foot. I mean as big as the end of my finger there and I'm bleeding like a stuck pig. And George says, "I'm going to beat you this time." And I said, "No. you're not gunna to beat me, I'm gunna to beat you." The problem was I couldn't take the glass out with my finger, but I was doing yoga at the time, and

I bent over and took it out with my teeth. So I left a trail of blood, but I beat him in the race.

"The funniest stories are about getting arrested for indecent exposure," David says. Here is one such story:

I used to work in Moscow those years as a brain researcher. . . . I was determined to run every road in Moscow, and the KGB must have thought I was a spy. I ran out into the countryside about 15 miles, and I was going to go to the end to the subway line and take the subway back. So I get out to the end of the line and I get on the subway, and I hear this voice, "Young man, young man" (in Russian), and it was the woman who was in charge of the subway, and she wouldn't let me on the train. So she called the police because I had no shoes, and the cops came and put me in a taxi, and I get down to the hotel and I say to the driver, "I'll bet you haven't seen this before, someone arrested for being barefoot." And he says, "Oh no, that's nothing. Last week the cops called me to the railroad station and there was a guy totally naked and drunk. Hey, you have clothes on, you know."

This account reflects the times and cultural sensibilities toward a barefoot runner:

Then in Soviet Georgia I used to run the route that Shevardnadze, the President, used to take in his limousine to go to work coming down off the mountain. This is in Tbilisi, Georgia. The guard house is along the route, and I would see the limousine pass. And one day when I'm running that route, the guard in the guard house sees me and he grabs me and he says, "The President can't see a barefoot man on my watch. You'll hide behind my guard house." So I had to hide there until the President passed and he says, "Now you can go, but don't ever come back."

David had two distinct phases to his running career. From his late 30s to his early 50s, he ran and raced with speed and efficiency, competing well in his age group and winning awards. In the New Haven 20K, a 12.4 mile race, he ran, at age 40, a personal best time of 1:22, at 6:40/mile. David ran from the 5k to the 20K but never did a marathon and explains, "I know the story of Pheidippides who runs the marathon to Athens to say the Persians have landed and then he drops dead. Who wants to do that?" In 1992, David moved to Paris to work for the United Nations as director of a project for world peace and found himself too busy to run for the next decade.

Retiring in 2001 at the age of 62, David returned to the U.S. and once again took up his barefoot running, albeit at a diminished pace. He met up with his running buddies a couple of days a week and was training three to five miles about every other day. It took several years before David returned to the racing scene, but by his late 60s the 5Ks were calling. Between 2008 and 2016 David averaged 10 to 15 competitions a year, totaling close to 100 races, and at age 77, he was still running a brisk 9:45/mile pace.

Until quite recently, David had not had any major medical problems. He has sustained common running injuries like plantar-fasciitis and Achilles tendinitis, but the setbacks have been short. In his 40s David did run into some trouble and says, "Once with the East Rock (running club) gang we ran 10 miles in deep snow, and I ran barefoot and got frost-bitten, so I don't do that anymore. I have one toe that still tells me when it gets cold because that's the toe that got frost-bite."

Then in June of 2016, at the Branford five-miler, I was waiting to photograph David at the finish line, but he never arrived. He had suffered an injury and had pulled himself off the race course. Turns out David had a meniscus tear of the left knee, and he was out of commission for the next four months. But by the end of September he had surgery to repair the knee and was back jogging about a month later. In mid-December David entered his first post-surgery race, the Christopher Martin's Christmas Run for Children, a large and well established 5K event in New Haven, Conn., where he won his 75-to-79 age division in a respectable 10:42/mile.

Keys to David's Success, Health, and Longevity

Running plays a prominent role in David's life and well-being. He points out, "It's become a priority for me, and I don't have a lot of competing priorities, because I'm retired and divorced. It's a kind of retirement thing, and I have the time to do it. . . . I'm on the computer all the time, and I need to get out, otherwise I'd be a couch potato if I didn't run." And David believes that running has a positive physiological effect on the heart muscle. He says:

> Your heart is strong when you run and your heart beats slower. Mine now is in the 50s and that's healthy. Humming birds don't live too long because they use up their heartbeats real fast. Elephants live a long time because they have a slow heart rate. If you have a slower heart rate, you're going to live longer.

David makes reference to diet as being a significant component of health and has this to say:

> I read a book a couple of years ago called the Anti-Cancer Book. The author found out that cancer cells need two things in order to reproduce: Glucose and vascularization (abnormal growth of blood vessels). Americans eat much too much glucose in white bread and sugar. As much as possible, I eat natural foods. I went to the farmer's market this morning and got fresh tomatoes, fresh Brussel-sprouts, good brown bread, fresh yogurt—good wholesome food."

David also makes the case for barefoot running as a major contributor to his success and longevity in road racing:

> You have to know how to run. Barefoot running helps because you run soft, you don't pound. People always complain they can't hear me catching up on them because I make no noise. . . . Your knees are slightly bent and you roll like this with your feet and you come down on your heel just slightly. There's no heel strike. So you run much softer with shorter strides, and you don't pound your joints.

David ended the interview with a few words from Satchel Paige, the great pitcher in the Negro Leagues: "Don't look back because something might be gaining on you."

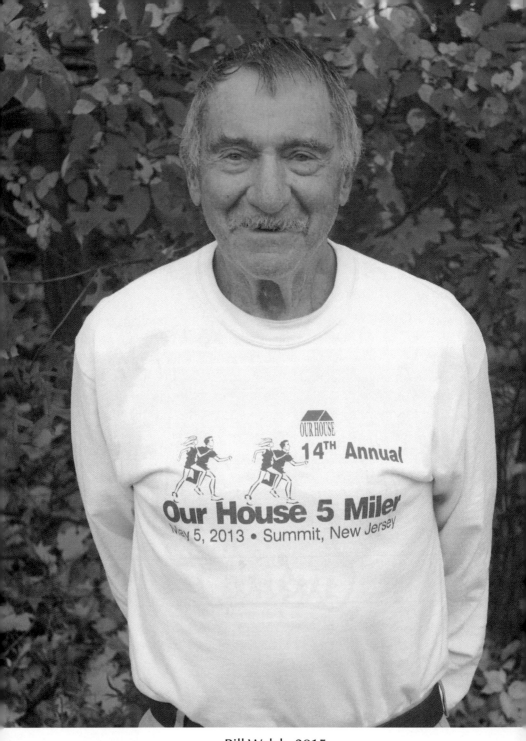

Bill Welch, 2015

Bill Welsh, 87
Running with Cancer

Bill was not a fast runner as a child. He says, "Well, it was about the fifth grade, and I found out I was too slow to even play tag with the girls, and the kids in grammar school made fun of me. I was the slowest. Turtles and snails could go by and I'd wave to them." But by middle school, Bill found that he was getting to school late and needed to jog part of the way not to be tardy. Soon he was jogging much of the mile back and forth to school each day and no longer had a sluggish reputation.

By high school, Bill was ready to challenge himself. His own school didn't have a running program, so he joined the cross-country team for Port Richmond High School in Staten Island, N.Y., and their illustrious coach, Mike Dwyer, who had inspired nine city championships. Although Bill could not officially compete at the meets, he still trained with the team and felt respected as one of their own. But it was the coach who lit the fire under Bill, a coach who also had the ability to run and compete as an older man at a high level. As Bill notes, "He had been competing, and I thought he was the oldest man that I ever saw, and my father would say, 'You let him beat you? He's an old man. He was running in 1918 with your Uncle Joe, and he was old then.'"

Under Coach Dwyer's tutelage, Bill thrived and developed into an exceptional runner. In 1946, his senior year—the year after World War Two ended—he ran in the Staten Island High School Championships and won the mile in 4:41, and six months later won the three-mile Staten Island Cross-County Championship in 15:58. Then, a month out of high school in an Amateur Athletic Union (AAU) development meet, Bill ran an astounding 4:27 mile in Queens. But this time he didn't win the race, as he points out. "Tommy Quinn ran like a 4:17. He was just working out. And I killed myself trying to stay close, and I stayed with him for three quarters, and then I died."

The Army Physical

Bill went for his military physical and recaptures the moment:

> I'm a non-vet because I failed the army physical after winning that race. I went up to White Hall Street, and the doctor with a stethoscope said, "You have a bad heart. Get on that cot, we will check you later." Well, I ran nine miles and won the championship the day before. You think you'd be a little tired too. Well, I fell asleep. When they first checked me my pulse was at 40. When I was asleep it was down to 34. . . . I wanted to go into the army because you could get your college paid for, and you come out commissioned and go into the academies. They said I had a bad heart. The text books said the normal heart has 72 beats per minute. This was in the 1940s . . . I kept working my heart rate down, and we were doing interval training, and it got down to 40. They didn't know about runners. My father said, "You better stop that running. How are we going to pay for college?" Well, I said, "I'll go see the school doctor," and the doctor said, "What the hell are you doing here?" I said, "I was told I have a bad heart." He said, "You just won the championships. Get your ass out of here."

Bill Welsh was born on July 5, 1929, in Staten Island, N.Y., and has lived his entire life on the island. Although he was rejected by the army for failing his physical, Bill was offered a full athletic scholarship to St. Frances College in Brooklyn. He was disappointed, however, with his performance: "My running in college wasn't good. It really stunk. I had one or two good races. I got to 4:24 in the mile by my senior year and that was it." But don't let Bill's modesty fool you. At age 20 he won the Junior National 15K Title, a 9.3 mile race in a blistering 49:28, averaging 5:20/mile. After college Bill began his teaching career, married his first wife, Lee, and they had three children.

Three Big Races of 1954

For Bill the best years were yet ahead. Just two months out of college in an AAU sponsored race in a park adjacent to Yankee Stadium, Bill broke his own personal best time in the mile in a sizzling 4:17, the same year Roger Bannister became the first to crack the four-minute mile and set a new world record. Then, at age 25 Bill had an extraordinary year, running in three races that distinguished his greatness and carved out a small niche in American road-racing history. First up was the National 25K Title, an AAU event in Pittsburgh. During the interview, Bill handed me an article entitled, "Ross Beats Welsh for National Title," and proceeded to tell how the race unfolded:

Ross went through five miles under 26 minutes, and this guy is burning the hills. In Pittsburgh they have a place called the Hill, Hill Street Blues, and it was tough, and what does Ross do? He starts wind-sprinting and he's trying to break me. And I said, "10 more miles to go, get smart," and I dropped back. I didn't go with him and he kept going. So his time was 1:24, and I broke 1:25.

Finishing within a minute of the Olympian, Browning Ross, was quite an achievement for Bill, considering the length of the race was 15.5 miles and took nearly an hour and a half to complete.

Next up was the New York City Metropolitan AAU 20K Championship. Bill passes me another article, this one from the New York Times dated November 1, 1954, with the heading, "Welsh Wins Title Run." Bill had traversed the course in a stunning 1:07:55, leaving behind such notables as the barefoot runner, Charlie Robbins, a two-time national champion in the marathon; Ted Corbitt, the first African American to compete in the Olympic marathon; and Joe Kleinerman, an excellent long-distance runner who helped found the New York Road Runners and establish the New York City Marathon.

Bill slips me another news item, the caption reading, "Bill Welsh Third in Senior National Run at Atlantic City," dated November 8, 1954. This was a 30K, 18.75 mile race for the American title and Bill had done superbly, running the race in 1:41:32, averaging 5:30/mile. In his own humble manner Bill states, "Look at the second-place man, Gordon Dickson, out of Canada. He trained in the mountains and was a two-time Olympian. Ross, the winner, has won at least 20 national championships and was also a two-time Olympian. Me, I went to Coney Island for my training."

In his late 20s, injuries took their toll and Bill was never the same runner. He says, "I had bone spurs that destroyed my career." Bill fought against the onslaught and resisted any change to his running routine:

> The doctor took the spur out, but he put me in a cast. Do you know how hard it is to run with a cast? On a cinder track that cast got chewed up. It just about looked like gangrene when I went back to him. He said, "What are you doing?" I said, "I just can't sit around." He put the cast back on and he said, "Just sit around."

Bill had bone spurs surgically removed on three separate occasions.

Over his 70-year running career, Bill believes he has competed in 1000 to 1500 races, from the 100 meter dash to the marathon. His best marathon was Atlantic City at age 32, in a fleet-footed 2:34, but Bill's preferred distance was the 15K to 20K, in the 9 to 13 mile range. In his 30s through his 60s, Bill continued to compete but says there were not as many races back then. Since he's 70, however, he thinks he has run in about 40 races a year.

After switching his teaching duties from history to physical education in 1973, Bill also began coaching at this time and has tutored many elite competitors, including Marty Walsh in the mile and two mile, Steve Moore in the shot put, and Larry Cimato in the half mile, all of whom have won New York City championship titles in their respective events. And he has also had the special pleasure to instruct Bill Jankunis, the Olympic high jumper. Bill is very proud of his coaching and the achievements of his athletes, and continues to volunteer as a coach for running clubs.

The Dreaded Diagnosis

Then, in 2010 came the feared diagnosis. At age 81, Bill got the news that he had amyloidosis, a rare form of cancer, which has required treatment of monthly chemotherapy infusions for the past six years. For his own sanity, Bill has continued to run and race during this challenging time: "I feel it's important I'm out here doing the running because I'm fighting cancer. You don't want to lose (tears well up in his eyes). My wife fought it for 27 years. Judy had breast cancer, both removed, kidney cancer, and uterine cancer." Judy passed away in 2011, the year after Bill's cancer diagnosis.

Seven Gold Medals

In 2014, Bill attended the USA Track & Field, New Jersey Masters Outdoor Championships and attempted to compete in seven different track and field events. At 85 years of age he entered the 100 meter dash, the 800 meter dash, the shot put, the discus throw, the long jump, the javelin throw, and the hammer throw, all in the hope of winning in each category. With seven gold medals at stake, Bill threw, leapt, and dashed to victory, an achievement that ought not to be minimized simply because he was the only one in his age group. How many other 85 year olds do you know who are skilled in the techniques and have the athletic ability to compete in these events? In another track and field championship meet, Bill's quest to win gold in ten events is portrayed in the documentary film entitled, Ten Gold Medals, directed and produced by James Guardino.

Keys to Bill's Success, Health, and Longevity

Bill says, "Number one is attitude. I can do this. I am a success at doing this." He mentions attempting to instill this "can do" spirit in the athletes he coaches. The sociability is another key that Bill considers essential. There are several ladies in their 80s that he likes to meet at the races. He says, "I enjoy the company of the women. I used to beat them in the races, and now we've changed places. And I yell to them as we go off, 'I can still see you.'" After the races they will all go to breakfast together and sometimes bring along one or two of the older gentlemen. Bill is on an 80s men's running team, and he enjoys their company too.

A cautionary note from Bill: "It's better to finish strong with a smile on your face than to go out too fast and walk and cry for what you wished you had done."

Patty Carton at the 5K Docs Race, 2016

Patty Carton, 78
Running Is Her Medicine

Pᴀᴛᴛʏ ʜᴀᴅ ꜰᴏᴜʀ ᴄʜɪʟᴅʀᴇɴ who needed to share the two family cars to get to high school. How was she going to get to the elementary school where she taught fourth through sixth grades? "Because it was snowing I couldn't ride my bike, so I decided to start running." Patty often ran the five miles back and forth to the school that winter. Once spring sprang, she was back on her bike commuting to work. But not for long: "I was hit by a car on the way to school, and my husband said, 'No more biking for you.' And then I took up running. So it started out of necessity."

By the time Patty was in her early 40s, it was the beginning of the running boom. She states, "In the late '70s and early '80s running wasn't that popular, especially for women. I felt a little self-conscious even running around the neighborhood." In the 1980s and '90s, Patty ran primarily for fitness and the good feeling it gave her. Then, around the time she turned 60, she discovered the pleasure of the racing circuit. One of Patty's favorite races, which she has done several times, is a four-miler in Prague, the Capitol of the Czech Republic, where she frequently visits with family. She says, "It's a lot of fun. You run through the cobble-stone streets along the river, and it's very picturesque." Another special event that Patty reminisces about is a three-generational race involving herself, her daughter, Kerry, and Kerry's three children, Erin, Peter, and Patrick. They have traditionally run the Stratford 5K together on Thanksgiving for the past 10 years.

Patty Carton was born on April 21, 1938, in Derby, Conn. After graduating from the University of Connecticut and receiving her master's in education from Southern Connecticut University, she went on to teach elementary school for the next 33 years. She married her first husband, Raymond, when she was 22, and they had three girls, Kerry, Susan, and Kristen, and a boy, Raymond Jr. Tragically, soon after the infamous 9/11 attack of 2001, her husband passed away from cancer at 66. It was at this time that Patty picked up the racing pace and, in the past decade or so, she has been averaging about 50 road races a year. I met Patty for the first time at the Autumn on the Sound 5K in October of 2015, and I distinctly remember how disappointed she was in her 11:23/mile pace. She was much more pleased with her New Haven 5K result of 10:44/mile from the previous month. Yet, Patty was never overly concerned with personal records and times. She was more interested in mingling with the other runners. She says, "I just enjoy the camaraderie, meeting people from all over Connecticut, all different ages, and everybody's friendly and nice. I'm not that competitive, because there's nobody to compete with." She's usually the only one in her age group.

Patty has a personal reason why she runs:

I had four children. Two of my daughters have passed away. Susan ran in New Haven, and she was dead within three weeks after that. She had breast cancer and was 48. This was just three years ago. She was a nurse practitioner, and she graduated from Columbia University as a mid-wife. Her husband is a physician, and they had all the medical knowledge and couldn't beat that breast cancer. My other daughter Kristen was an accountant. It was a bad storm, and her car hydro-foiled on her way home from work, and she was killed. That was 20 years ago, when she was 30. . . . So those are two good reasons for me to get up and run every day. It centers me. You have to learn to move forward. . . . I don't take any medication whatsoever. My medicine is running. So I run with a purpose to keep myself going forward. You know, I have other children and I have grandchildren.

Keys to Patty's Success, Health, and Longevity

Patty's attitude toward running is easygoing and non-competitive. She says, "I don't push it. I just relax and go along. And I collect golf balls along the way, so I'm not timing myself. I've never timed myself, and I don't think of it as training. I just think of it as part of my daily life." This outlook on running is also the reason Patty feels she has never sustained a running injury. In addition, she relishes the human contact that comes with racing and the running community: "I've met so many great people, like I've met you now. The sociability is great. I think that's very important, especially as we get older and we've retired. That's what I think is a key to longevity."

Besides running as a major pastime, Patty and her current husband, Richard, love to travel the world and have been to such diverse places as Vietnam, Cambodia, South Africa, India, Egypt, Argentina, Peru, Ecuador, and throughout Europe, spending at least a month in each locale.

Patty had a few parting words: "I'm just happy to be running a race and be standing up at the end."

Herman Bershtein at the 5K Docs Race, 2016. His bib number
reflects his age.

Herman Bershtein, 91

Running, Racing, and Working as a Full-Time Attorney

Hᴇʀᴍᴀɴ ᴡᴀs ᴛᴏᴏ ʙᴜsʏ to meet with me. Finally, after some serious arm twisting over the phone he relented, but I would have to wait six weeks before conducting the interview. He made it clear that his work took priority and he was already down one attorney. Founding his law practice in 1954 in Hamden, Conn., specializing in personal-injury law, Herman continues to work six days a week in the original building along with his law partners, Richard, Joy, and Jan, his three children. There is a conspicuous sign out front that you cannot miss, announcing your arrival to the "Bershtein Bershtein Bershtein Law Center."

In tribute to Herman's turning 90, there was a surprise ending to the 5K race on Labor Day in New Haven, Conn., five days after his 90th birthday. As Herman remembers it:

> At the end of the race all of the runners that had finished were lined up. And as I went up a little hill at Connecticut State University, they had the music on through a loud speaker, and they were playing a song of Rocky Balboa. He was the boxer in that Stallone movie. In the movie he was running up the steps in Philadelphia and he was punching his way along and getting his legs and his arms moving like a fighter. And the loud speaker played that song just for me.

And all the other finishing runners were lined up, and the music was blaring away, and just as Rocky was punching his way along, so I started punching my way as I was going through the finishing area, with the other runners on both sides all clapping and yelling, and the music is blaring away. It was really exciting.

Herman Bershtein was born on September 2, 1925, in Hamden, Conn. While a freshman at Yale University in 1943, he enlisted in the army during World War Two and became a second lieutenant assisting in the training of troops. While preparing to be sent to the Pacific arena, Herman took amphibious instruction in San Diego, Calif., which entailed climbing over the side of the ship on rope ladders with fixed bayonets at night. One time he was accidentally clipped by a soldier's bayonet on the neck and was bleeding profusely. Herman says that was as close to combat as he got, and that he was never sent overseas.

After establishing his law practice, Herman married Shirley in 1956, and they moved into the house he still lives in today and had three children. Then about 20 years later, at 50, Herman had what he describes as a mini-stroke. Up to that point he had been depending on golf for his exercise, so his doctor suggested he try something more strenuous like jogging. Herman, therefore, started running around the neighborhood, and his son, Richard, who played varsity baseball at Yale, joined him on runs at the nearby university track. Soon after, when his son was at Columbia University Law School, Richie would sign the two of them up for races in Central Park in Manhattan. Yet, at this time in his 50s, Herman was running primarily for exercise and relaxation.

Beginning in his early 60s, Herman became more serious about his running and racing. Once Richie returned home and took a position in his father's law firm, the two of them began to train together. They would work at the office until 6:00 p.m., go out and do an hour run, and then return to work for an hour. Sometimes they did interval speed work at the Yale track with a group. This running togetherness lasted until Richie got married and had his first child. At that point Herman was on his own and became less concerned about speed and his times.

Ran a Marathon at 81

Altogether, Herman has completed about 900 races, averaging 30 races a year for 30 years. He has run 19 marathons, including the Boston and New York City Marathons several times each, Rocky Neck in East Lyme, Conn., numerous times, and the Hartford, Chicago, Rhode Island, and Bridgeport Marathons. His last Boston Marathon was in 1999, which he ran at 74, and the New York City Marathon in 2000, at age 75. Not known for exceptional speed, Herman's best Marathon was New York City in 4:32, when he was 63, although he is quite pleased with his best 5K in 7:30/mile, also in his early 60s. By the way, Herman's final marathon was Rock Neck; he was 81 years of age. To run 26.2 miles at that age is truly an extraordinary achievement.

Presently, Herman is still racing nearly every weekend except in the cold months. He now limits his running to twice a week, including a race on the weekend. For cross-training purposes, he includes two days of weight training and a day of swimming per week. Luckily, Herman has had few medical setbacks. One problem that affects him and his joints is gout, for which he takes medication. In February, 2016, Herman also suffered a stroke, slightly compromising his vision. After four days in the hospital, he spent another three weeks at home recuperating. Soon, Herman was back to work and walking, and in two months after the stroke, he was back in the races. His current system is to walk the uphills, run the downhills, and alternate running and walking the flats.

At 89, however, Herman took a fall while running in the Madison Turkey Trot on Thanksgiving Day. As he recalls it:

> I was notorious for sprinting, let's say, the last 100 to 200 yards. You see the finish and you sprint, and I would pass anywhere between eight to ten people, okay. I had a kick. And last year at this Madison race I could see the end and I said to myself, okay, it's time to sprint. Somehow my mind said "Go" and my legs said "No", and I went face down. I had a few cuts and bruises and I'm bloody and everything, and the official said, "You're done," and I said, "Like hell I am, I'm finishing," and I did.

Keys to Herman's Success, Health, and Longevity

For Herman the primary ingredient for a healthful life is physical activity. He states:

> The key is the exercise, that's the real key. You know, you sit at a desk for eight hours, six hours, you really get sluggish. Your mind isn't clear. Getting out there and running, gee, it's like rejuvenating . . . There are many times I don't have the time, but you have to make the time. You have to go out there."

Herman also points out, "I think my kids are a key to my success." Richie ran and raced with his father for a good 15 years, while Joy cheers him on at the events from the sidelines. In conclusion, Herman believes in the notion of "fresh legs"—that starting out running later in life has minimized the impact on his body. He says, "I think there is a lot of storage of energy in my legs that had yet to be expended. By not using it initially in earlier days, I had a lot left."

Toward the end of the interview, Herman reminded me that he resides by himself in his home and said, "I live alone and I'm available too, so tell your girlfriends, okay?"

Tony Medeiros, 85
Running after By-Pass, Pacemaker, and Replaced Knee

TONY RAN A MARATHON in Warwick, N.Y., on November 12, 1995, at 64 years of age. He illuminates how treacherous it was:

> When the race started it was unbelievably cold. It was so cold I had to have a mask covering my face, and then it started to snow. It got so bad that you had to make sure you were seeing someone in front of you so you wouldn't lose your way. If you let them get too far in front of you, then you'd have to watch for footprints. Then you'd have to pick up the pace so at least you'd see someone. It was just about a blizzard. It got to the point that not too many people after me finished because they pulled them off the course. And when I did finish, I went back to the motel and I got in the shower and just sat there. I must have sat there for a half an hour, just sitting there trying to warm up my body.

Tony ran between 20 and 25 marathons, but this one in Warwick was perhaps the most formidable of all. He didn't remember his time or whether he placed in his age group, but was just grateful to have finished and to soak in hot water and thaw out.

Tony Medeiros was born on September 22, 1931, in Fall River, Mass. After high school he joined the army and was stationed in Germany outside of Munich as a part of the occupying force from 1949

Tony Medeiros at the Chilly Chili Run 5K Run, 2016. His bib number reflects his age.

to 1952. Soon after his military discharge at age 22, Tony apprenticed as a tool and die maker, and for the next 40 years made that his career, moving up to shop foreman, plant manager, and, with his final company, sales manager before retiring at 65. He married Marcie in 1955, they had two daughters and a son, and have been joyfully married for 61 years.

Earlier in his life, Tony had been physically active playing soccer and boxing, and while bringing up the kids, he always did the yardwork. Then, when Tony was 51, he went to see a physician because of his chronic sore throat. He had been a smoker since being discharged from the army, and he took the doctor's advice to stop smoking, and the sore throat went away. But Tony began to put on weight and, as a response, he started walking and, soon after that, jogging and running.

It wasn't long before Tony hit the racing circuit. He demonstrated some ability in just his second race, a two-miler in 12:57, at 6:29/mile, a competition in which he beat and embarrassed his two younger friends who had brought him to the event. At 53, by the end of his second year of running, Tony entered the New York City Marathon, the first of many marathons and 40 to 45 half marathons. His best New York City Marathon was in 3:39 in 1987 at age 56, and his best 10K was the Glastonbury Apple Run in 1986 in 44:45, at 7:13/mile, at 55. Tony's final marathon was in Duluth, Minn., in 1996 at age 65.

For 12 years, between the ages of 53 and 65, Tony averaged around 35 races a year, totaling close to 400 races. He was training up to 60 miles a week for his marathons and half marathons and running five to six days a week. He used some speed work, hill runs, and long easy runs up to 15 miles.

In 1996, Tony was training for another marathon when he felt pain in his left knee and had to stop running. To address the problem he had arthroscopic surgery to remove some cartilage and was told by the doctor not to run anymore. Tony gave it six months to heal and tried running again, but the discomfort was too great and he quit. At that point he stopped running and started putting on the pounds.

Then on September 10, 2001, the day before the World Trade Center attack, while vacationing in Portugal with his wife, Tony suffered severe pain in his back. Upon his return he went to see a cardiologist who informed Tony that he'd had a minor heart attack and there was a blockage requiring surgery. He spent a total of 19 days in the hospital, and during his stay had triple by-pass surgery, and four days later had a pacemaker implanted. Considering these major medical procedures and the chronic pain in his left knee, the prospects for Tony ever to run again looked bleak indeed.

In 2010, nearly a decade after the heart and pacemaker surgeries, Tony initiated his search for an orthopedic doctor who could treat his knee problem. The first physician advised Tony to have knee replacement surgery and firmly stated he would not be able to run anymore. Feeling disappointed, he sought a second opinion but essentially got the same result. Yet, he didn't give up. With resolute determination he pursued a third opinion, and this time the doctor stated, "You're a perfect candidate for a partial," and went on to describe the knee replacement procedure using titanium. Tony then popped the big question. "Will I be able to run?" The doctor responded, "I don't see why you can't. Yah, if you do little running, I see nothing wrong with that." That was music to Tony's ears.

Back in the Race at 80

Tony was up walking the hallways of the hospital the day after his partial knee replacement and was discharged later that afternoon. As soon as he was home he was out walking and within four to six weeks was jogging. Six months after surgery Tony was back in the races, and as a gesture of thanks sent his surgeon a picture of himself with one of his recent trophies. After a hiatus of 16 years, Tony was back in the game and doing what he loves to do. For the past five years he has been running and racing with regularity, averaging 25 races a year, and those age group awards keep piling up.

Tony is now 85 and still going strong. But that doesn't mean he won't ease up on his competition once in a while, as Tony at age 83 illustrates in this 5K race:

There was this young lady, and she had a daughter maybe seven or eight, and the daughter kept stopping and the mother kept trying to egg her on. And I followed behind them for a while, and I started to pass them, and I said to the little girl, "You're not going to let an old man like me beat you, are you?" And I says, "I want you to pick them legs up." Well, her and I kept the pace going and the mother kept looking back and smiling, so we kept going. And just as we get close to the finish line, I just backed off and let her go, and then we all did high-5s, and I said, "See, I knew you could beat me." She figured, "I'm not going to let this old man beat me."

Tony was one of my inspirations for writing this book. I originally met him at a 5K race in 2013 and was amazed by his story. How anyone at 81 years of age could be running after triple by-pass surgery, an implanted pacemaker, and a partially replaced knee just seemed unfathomable.

Keys to Tony's Success, Health, and Longevity

Tony points out:

Happiness is important. I have basically no stress whatsoever, okay. I have my wife, who I've been married to for over 60 years. I have two daughters and a son, and I have six grandchildren. I don't worry. Some people just worry about everything. I don't. You can't let every little thing bother you. It'll take care of itself. And you have to take life as it is and make the best of it.

Advice from Tony: "Turn off the TV and go out for a long walk."

Sylvie Kimché, 2015

Sylvie Kimché, 70

Fastest Woman Her Age in NYC Tri-State Region

Roberta and Sylvie knew each other well and were members of the Milrose team until one day Roberta switched her allegiance to another running club. Sylvie felt betrayed that her running friend had deserted their team for that of a competitor. And, on top of that, Roberta got faster. As a result, they became arch rivals, as Sylvie reveals:

> You have to understand, I'm very competitive, and I used to beat Roberta all the time. Then, she quit the team, and she went to train with another team, and she started getting much better. Then, in the Boston Marathon she beat me, and I was not happy about that. . . . So I'm at the start of the New York City Marathon in 1987, and I'm feeling pretty good. Then, I think it was about mile eight on that big avenue that goes into Brooklyn, and, suddenly, Roberta passes me and I think, "Oh no, not again." And I thought I needed more energy, so I started drinking Gatorade, which I never do, and I got the worst stomach ache. Then, at about mile 20 the stomach ache went away, and I started feeling good, and I started passing people, and that made me feel even better. And in those days the marathon course was going up 102nd Street, which was an uphill. And who do I see towards the top of the hill? It's Roberta. And I thought, "Oh my God, she must be struggling because I'm catching up on her." I

137

thought she would be far ahead of me. And so that gave me another boost, and sure enough I passed her. And I felt, okay, I got my revenge today.

This anecdote reflects not only Sylvie's competitive spirit, but her skill and ability in the sport of road racing. She ran this marathon in an impressive personal best time of 3:07, at a 7:08/mile pace. In fact, besides running her first New York City Marathon in 3:26, Sylvie ran her remaining five marathons between 3:07 and 3:14, all in her early 40s.

Sylvie Kimché was born on December 11, 1946 in Nyons, France. From an early age she had an interest in a variety of sports. "As a kid I was always a tomboy," she says. "I was doing basketball, volleyball, handball, soccer, and swimming." Sylvie also exhibited an athletic talent in track and field as a sprinter, in the high jump, and making the French national championships in the long jump at age 14. But above all, Sylvie was an outstanding skier. While attending Grenoble University in France to study languages, she says her real interest was in Alpine skiing, and she competed in the downhill, special slalom, and giant slalom events, and was nationally ranked in all three categories. No doubt, Sylvie was a versatile athlete before finding her running niche.

In the 1970s, Sylvie was employed by Club Med as a custom designer and eventually was put in charge of entertainment, while also working intermittently as a sweater designer in southern France. By 1979 at age 32, Sylvie moved to New York City. To keep her weight down, she joined a local gym and ran on the treadmill several times a week. Then, in her late 30s, she met a man who became her boyfriend and who was a marathon runner. Sylvie thought, "Well, if I take up running, it will get us closer, so I took up running and marathoning. It didn't keep the relationship going, but that's when I became a real runner." Sylvie was now 40, and within a few years, she would run all six of her marathons and set all her PRs (personal records). Take a look at these awe-inspiring numbers: A mile in New York City in 5:10; a 5K in Albany in 18:01 at 5:48/mile; a 10K in Pittsburgh in 38:19 at 6:10/mile; and a 10-miler in Washington, D.C., in 1:02, at 6:18/mile. But a sudden stroke of bad luck put an abrupt end to her road racing. At age 44, Sylvie suffered a back injury that kept her out of the running loop for two years, and it took several more years before she could build back her training and confidence.

12-Time Winner of the NYRR Runner of the Year Award

By age 50, Sylvie was back in full swing and running well, winning the acclaimed New York Road Runners (NYRR) Runner of the Year award for her 50-to-54 age group, and again at age 55 for the 55-to-59 age group. But she spent much of the time in her 50s traveling for work and living in Columbus, Ohio, while commuting to New York City. She was a fashion designer and production manager, traveling throughout Asia and Europe. Apart from the two years she won this prestigious award, her work took priority and her running was secondary. "Then, when I turned 60 and retired," Sylvie says, "I thought, 'Now I have time to train.' I was not working anymore, and I didn't have to travel all over the world for my job." This gave Sylvie the opportunity to focus on her running and racing, and she took full advantage of it, winning her age group in every race throughout her 60s, except two. For her momentous achievements, Sylvie has accepted the NYRR Runner of the Year award 10 times in her 60s, and 12 times overall.

Being part of a fellowship of runners and, in particular, an active member of the Central Park Track Club (CPTC), has given Sylvie a sense of belonging. She points out:

> You know, I don't have a family anymore. The running club is my family. I have one sister, and my parents passed away years ago. I was never married and never had kids, and my sister was never married and had no kids. So it's just her and me. And since I decided to make my life in America, it's only me. So the running community is like a big family to me. I know I'm going to see people I've known for years and years, and they are a part of my social network. . . . So the club gave me this award, and I have to say that I was really moved because the whole team stood up to clap for me. And I felt so good about that, because I was just coming back from Paris, and my sister was not doing well and was in a lot of pain. But it was

such a great feeling to get this award from my teammates, and to feel the camaraderie and love and the recognition of my accomplishments.

Sadly, Sylvie's sister, Danièle, passed away from a long bout with cancer on July 21, 2016, but the running community continues to sustain and inspire Sylvie.

What Sets Sylvie Apart

Frankly, it's the focus, intensity, and effort put into other physical endeavors that separates Sylvie from most of us runners. For instance, 25 years ago after her back injury, a friend of her mother's taught her yoga exercises to strengthen the muscles in the back. For the last quarter century Sylvie has faithfully followed this yoga regimen after every race, and she includes stretching and calisthenics like pushups and sit-ups as well.

But that's just the beginning. Let Sylvie tell you what else she does for cross-training:

That's the part that makes me different. Instead of just running I do other things. In fact, I retired at the end of May, 2007, to go on a 40-day bike tour. That was called Chasing the Great Divide. I was going from the bottom of New Mexico all the way to Jasper, Canada, going up and down the Continental Divide as many times as possible. . . . Well, now-a-days since I've turned 60, I think that's part of the reason why I have longevity, because I'm not only running, I'm doing other things to keep me strong—like biking. I spent two months this year on bike tours, and last year in 2014, I did about the same. In 2010, I went across the county on a bike tour from Hobuck Beach in Washington State to Bar Harbor, Maine, and that took us 58 days. And I go hiking too. I've gone on hiking tours in the Himalayas. I've gone to Bhutan, Nepal, Peru, and Patagonia in Chile. I've gone to high altitudes, like when I was in Nepal and I climbed Saribung Peak, which is at 21,300 feet. So I would say I've done about five to eight weeks of hiking every year since I'm 60. The other thing I need to mention is, in the past two years, I've been going up and down the steps of my building or wherever I am. Last year I averaged going up 41 floors per day. I never take elevators. I climb steps, and I think that's part of my training to stay strong. So when I'm running up a hill, I'm thinking, "Okay, you can do that. You're climbing up steps all the time, you can run the hill." I also walk everywhere, and I don't take the subway. I walk over 25 miles per week, and I walk fast. I think that's the reason why I'm strong, because I keep exercising all the time. Basically, my whole life is an exercise. And it prevents me from getting injured because I don't do so much running.

For the past decade Sylvie has spent about three months of the year on hiking and biking tours.

Keys to Sylvie's Success, Health, and Longevity

Sylvie's cross-training keeps her fit. She comments, "I keep active and do a lot of exercise, but I don't run a lot because the pounding is what kills you when you get older. So by running less, but doing more other types of exercise to keep me strong—that's what has saved me." Sylvie also believes being active in her childhood has helped her develop a solid base and says, "I started as a tomboy. I built strong bones, strong muscles, strong ligaments doing all the sports I did." And she thinks that starting her running later in her 40s has helped to prolong her running career. She points out, "Between 20 and 40, I didn't run much. Basically I was doing other sports like water-skiing, snow-skiing, and scuba-diving. I've been an athlete all my life but not a runner, so I didn't have the pounding that takes a toll on your body." Sylvie suggests that another possible key to her health is her daily use of two over-the-counter substances, glucosamine and chondroitin, which were recommended to her by a chiropractor in Hong Kong about 20 years ago for joint protection.

Sylvie's advice: "Keep moving. Whatever you do, keep moving. When you're going up on an escalator keep moving, keep walking."

A few final words from Sylvie: "In life you have to step up to the line. In everything you do, step up to the line."

Joe Riccio, 2015

Joe Riccio, 82
Has Run 79 Marathons

Joe was in his early 40s before he began running. This is how it happened:

> What inspired me to run was, I had developed bad habits, drinking and eating late at night. I gained a lot of weight. I got on the scale and it said 202 pounds, and I was overweight and fat. With that, I gave it all up. No more drinking, and I went on a strict steak and salad diet. I also decided to do some exercising, and I went out for a run and I couldn't complete one mile.

But that got Joe going, and he has been running and racing ever since. For six years Joe ran for conditioning and enjoyment, but by age 48, he had discovered the racing circuit. Overall, Joe estimates he has competed in 1400 races over the past four decades, and, during that time, has demonstrated his elite status among masters runners. Take a gander at these stats: In his 50s he ran a 5K in 17:45, under 6:00/mile pace, a 10K in 38:30, at 6:12/mile, and a half marathon in 1:24, at 6:28/mile. As Joe bluntly states, "I was virtually unbeatable as a 60-year-old. I was still doing 19s for a 5K, and nobody passes me the last quarter-mile of a race, and to this day I fight for that." Joe also enjoys doing annual road races. He has completed the New Haven 20K, 34 out of the past 36 years, and has run the Manchester Road Race the past 14 years.

His love of the marathon is what distinguishes Joe from other exceptional masters runners. He has completed 79 marathons, including New York City three times, Boston five times, the Marine Corp 15 times, Chicago three times, Philadelphia eight times, Baltimore twice, and many others. Yet, his favorite was always the Vermont City Marathon in Burlington, Vt., which he ran 25 times, the last time at age 79 in 5:20, and his personal best in 3:10, at 7:16/mile. Amazingly, Joe had run the Marine Corp Marathon just a week before he ran each of his three New York City Marathons. I asked Joe how that was possible, and he simply said, "I recover quickly. I am blessed, John."

Joe Riccio was born on July 29, 1934, in New Haven, Conn. He played basketball in high school and ran cross-country in college, but after graduating from Providence College in 1955, he put running aside to start his career and a family. With a master's degree in education, Joe taught middle and high school for 20 years, married his first wife, and had three children. To keep active he played in softball and basketball leagues in his 20s and 30s, but still managed to put on the pounds. He explains, "All those sports were a keg of beer after every ball game. It was all diminishing returns."

Beyond his passion for competing, Joe adores the races for the human interaction. As he points out, "Camaraderie, that's the whole thing. There's no point going to a road race and just jumping out of your car, jumping in line, doing the race, jumping back in your car, and going home without talking to people. I'm there until everyone goes home. You mingle with people." Joe has been president of the Warren Street Social and Athletic Club for the past 20 years and continues to run with this group. He says, "And I take care of them like they're my flock."

Hamstrings and hernias have been the only medical hurdles for Joe. In his 60s a hamstring injury kept him from running for three months. Then, a double hernia was diagnosed about six years ago, and Joe was confronted with his aversion to doctors and hospitals. He remarks, "I was convinced to go to the doctor and I was petrified. . . . Then the other fear kicked in, if they were going to keep me overnight as an inpatient. I was planning an escape. They were not going to keep me there, and I was not going to stay overnight." As it turned out, Joe was released the same day and his fears were relieved. He took eight weeks to recover completely and then was back to running on the roads. More recently Joe has had some knee discomfort. His solution is to stretch and warm up by jogging for about 10 minutes before he can fully stride.

The Chilly Chili Run

For the past 22 years, Joe has found a new niche in the running community—being the race director of nine local Connecticut road races. Catering to the older runners is a characteristic of these events. They promote age groups in the 60s, 70s, 80s, and 90+, often using five-year increments, and in Doc's Race free entry for those over 65. But the cream of the crop is the 5K Chilly Chili Run, best known for its chilly weather on New Year's Day and tasty chili to keep you warm after the race. On the event application it states: "The Showcase for 90-year-old Legends Who Run, Compete, Inspire!" Joe wines and dines the 90-year-old runners and their spouses over dinner on New Year's Eve, the evening before the race, and then puts them up in the Marriott Hotel overnight, all at his own expense. I had the pleasure to attend the Chilly Chili Run of 2016, and three of the 90-year-old runners featured in this book ran in that race.

Keys to Joe's Success, Health, and Longevity

Joe notes, "It's in the genes." His father lived to 88 and his mother to 97. Also, Joe's run training has been paramount: "You've got to be faithful to your training, otherwise you're going to be a failure. You can't take your conditioning and put it in a bottle and put it on the shelf, and when you run again you take a sip of that." Perhaps the most critical factor is Joe's all-encompassing passion for the sport: "The important thing is I am always connected with road racing, whether I'm racing it, or directing it, or just being a spectator, or a volunteer, I'm always connected with it."

Finally, Joe reflects, "There is a spiritual aspect of running too. I know for me it gives me an inner peace."

Bill Borla, 2015

Bill Borla, 76
Sets Record for 5th Avenue Mile

THIS WAS A RACE FOR THE AGES, and Mr. Borla, at age 60, was poised and primed as he approached the starting line, with picturesque Central Park off to the right. Bill catapults us into the race:

> So here we go, we take off, and here I am alongside Sid Howard. The two of us are out ahead of the pack. Sid, I knew was an 800 meter indoor world champion at one time in his 60s . . . So there we are out front, you know. Oh boy, here's Sid next to me and then he drops back a little bit, because that's how he ran. I remembered he would stay right off the shoulder of the front guy. So we got to within 100 meters of the finish and all of a sudden Sid throws it into his finishing kick, and he had a heck of a kick. He went by me almost as if I was standing still. But fortunately for me I was able to drop the hammer myself, and I think, "Come on, this is the Big Apple, take advantage of this opportunity." So I'm going like crazy, and I catch him, and I finally go by him, and I nip him at the end. So there is a crowd of people there and everyone is yelling. And my friend, Jerry LeVasseur, couldn't see us, but he heard the noise, and he says, "What happened, did Sid beat you?" And I said, "No, I beat him." And he said, "What, you beat Sid Howard, you out-kicked Sid Howard?" And I said, "I guess so."

It was September 23, 2000, and this was the 5th Avenue Mile in the middle of Manhattan with some of the finest male competitors in their 60s racing against each other in one of the most prestigious New York City road races sponsored by the New York Road Runners club. Bill had indeed nipped Sid at the finish line in a winning time of 5:06, but in the process they both had broken the race record for the 60-to-69 age group. Records, though, are made to be broken, and the very next year, Vic Heckler of Chicago set a new mark under the five-minute mile.

Bill Borla was born on March 1, 1940 in Torrington, Conn., where he has lived for most of his life. After graduating from college, he took a job with the Department of Transportation in Connecticut as a civil engineer specializing in highway planning. Around that time Bill married Mary Ann, and they had three girls and a boy.

Keeping active, Bill had played competitive basketball in high school, college, and men's leagues in his 20s, but had not yet been bitten by the running bug. Then, he went on a three-day backpacking trip in the Adirondack Mountains and had this to say: "And on the way up this mountain I just completely ran out of gas. My brain was telling my foot to move, but I couldn't get my foot off the ground. I was just done, and I thought I was in pretty good shape." This happenstance provided the incentive for Bill to try running. He thought that if he ran, he could get in better shape for these strenuous hiking trips.

Thus, at age 30, Bill began on his running adventure. After work he ran around a cemetery near his home up to three to six miles a day, five to six days a week. Often his runs took place after dark, but as long as the moon was out, or there were clouds to reflect the light, he could manage to see. The challenge was when the skies were clear and he had to be especially careful on those nights. This initial phase of Bill's running career lasted for 14 years.

By the time Bill was 44, he had become more serious about his running and training and was ready for the races. At age 46 he won the Torrington Road Race, a five-miler, averaging 5:45/mile on a very hot and humid day, and was already exhibiting his potential as an elite runner. Using the Arthur Lydiard training program, Bill incorporated a variety of running techniques from speed work with intervals and time trials, to hill repeats and long, easy runs, and, in this way, his speed and endurance were enhanced. By his late 50s, Bill was hitting his stride, quite literally, and was emerging as a nationally acclaimed, age-group runner.

Bill Breaks National Record for the 5K

For the past 32 years, Bill believes he has competed in 12 to 15 races a year, totaling around 400 races from the 800 meters to the marathon. In almost all of these races he would come in first in his age division and win awards, which didn't always please his wife. At the Litchfield Hills Road Race 7-miler, Bill would win his age group each year and come home with these attractive granny clocks. But he points out, "My wife got tired of it and she said, 'Don't bring home those clocks anymore. Come in second and win a wristwatch.'"

On May 27, 2005, at the Moonlight Run in New Milford, Conn., Bill ran faster than anyone his age had ever done in the United States. In this 3.1-mile race at 65 years of age, Bill ran a blistering 18:12, in a 5:52/mile pace, and, in so doing, set a new American record in the 5K for the 65-to-69 age division. Ten years later, as of my interview with Bill in December of 2015, this USA Track & Field record still stands.

Some of Bill's personal best times for specific age categories are astounding and deserve special attention. Take, for example, the Mid May Classic in Fairfield, Conn., a four-mile race that Bill ran in a torrid 22:24, a 5:36/mile pace at age 60. Then there is the Ridgefield Half Marathon, in Ridgefield, Conn., which he ran in a blazing 1:24, a 6:27/mile pace at age 65. At the Simsbury River Run in Simsbury, Conn., a 10K event, Bill ran an electrifying 40:22, a 6:30/mile pace at age 70. And, although he never put much emphasis on the marathon, Bill still managed to achieve a time of 3:07 in the Ocean State Marathon in Providence, R.I., at 59 years of age.

USA Track & Field Runner of the Year

Demonstrating world class speed, Bill was encouraged to compete on the national level by his good friend Jerry LeVasseur. As Bill explains:

Jerry was the motivating force on all this stuff. . . . Well, one time I got a call from Jerry. He says, "Bill, you owe me $350." I said, "No, I don't Jerry, I think we are even with all the stuff we've done and everything." He says, "No, this is for your plane ticket." I said, "What?" He says, "Yah, you're going out to the national championships in Eugene, Oregon. That's your round-trip plane ticket." So I was stunned for a few seconds, and I didn't know what to say, and I said to him, "Wooow, when is that?"

For about a dozen years, Bill and Jerry, along with Jerry's wife and another gentleman named Phil, a World War Two, Iwo Jima survivor, would often attend the USA Track & Field (USATF) National Championships and Senior Olympic Games together. Bill felt that going to these meets was also a great way to see part of the country. For instance, at a national competition in St. George, Utah, they got to visit Zion National Park, Bryce Canyon, and Las Vegas. And Bill always enjoyed the sociability over meals and sightseeing together, along with meeting the other runners. But, no doubt, the excitement of the competition was the primary draw, and Bill did exceptionally well at these national races. The USATF acknowledged Bill's outstanding road-running performance by bestowing upon him the Runner of the Year award in 2003 for the 60-to-64 age group, when he was age 63, and again in 2005 for the 65-to-69 age group when he was 65 years of age. These are remarkable accomplishments.

Racing with a World Record Holder

The national races he ran with Jan Holmquist, who possesses American and world records in her age group, were especially momentous to Bill. While Jan was in her late 60s and Bill in his early 70s, they each ran the anchor in their 4-by-1600 meter race on their respective relay teams at a national championship event in Boston. Although the men's and women's teams did not directly compete against each other, nevertheless, the teams were on the race course at the same time. Bill vividly remembers Jan just in front of him and attempting in vain to catch this fleet-footed woman. Jan was simply too fast for Bill.

Then, at a USATF 10K National Championship race in 2013, in Denham, Mass., Bill had a chance at redemption. He recalls the occasion:

So the race starts out, and somewhere right in the beginning I passed Jan, and I thought, okay, you know, I'll see her at the end of the race and we'll chat. So we keep running and we're getting close to the end and I feel someone coming up behind me. I can hear the footsteps and the breathing, and this person pulled up alongside me, and I look over there, and it's Jan. What the heck, and she starts pulling away from me. She was putting the pedal to the metal, pulling ahead of me. . . . I said, "Oh no, not this again." It took me everything I had to catch up to her, because I didn't want her to beat me again. And I think there are maybe 50 meters to go or so, and I started to go a little ahead of her. I was going by her because I thought she was running out of gas. Then I reached down and grabbed her hand so we could go across the line holding hands. And the announcer I knew from Torrington, and he announces, "Jan Holmquist age 70, and runner Bill Borla, 73, coming across together."

Bill thinks Jan broke her own American record in this race and that he came in second in his age group.

Although Bill still follows the same training regimen, he has cut his mileage in half. In his 50s and 60s, Bill was running 50 miles a week, but now in his mid-70s, he runs in the 25-to-30-mile range with less intense speed and hill work. Luckily, Bill has remained free of major injuries for his entire running career, although at age 72 he was diagnosed with prostate cancer, underwent treatment, and took a break from running during that time.

What has running meant to Bill? "I think that's part of why I've really enjoyed my life. I've had a good life, and that was a big part of it, you know, because I got so much enjoyment and so much fun out of all that." As part of that fun, Bill describes his participation in relay races, like the 200-mile relay in New Hampshire with 12 runners, each running three legs of the race. But the relay race that most touches Bill's heart is the annual family event at the Hartford

Marathon, with each family member running between three and seven miles. Bill originally thought of this idea to celebrate his daughter, Wendy, who has cerebral palsy and is now 48. She likes pink, so the family relay team is named the Pink Lady. As a family, they have completed the Hartford Marathon six times in a row, with up to five members and three generations participating in each race.

Keys to Bill's Success, Health, and Longevity

Retiring early from his 34-year career as a civil engineer gave Bill an edge: "I retired fairly young at 57, and was able to concentrate more on the running. I can take a nap in the afternoon, you know, I'm more flexible in what I can do. The additional stresses on you, it takes that away from you." Being adequately prepared before and after a run is crucial to Bill. He says, "I make sure I warm up and cool down and stretch. I found out from watching the Kenyans. When you watch the Kenyans warming up, you can walk faster than what they're doing. But watch out after they get warmed up a little bit." Having good training partners, Bill believes, has made a big difference. He states, "When you train with somebody who is as fast as you are, you naturally go faster." He trained with his friend Bob Sieller twice a week for 20 years and frequently with groups of runners on the weekends. Another key for Bill is his passion for the sport: "I have an enthusiasm for running. I love to get out and run, and I have this beautiful area I run in. It's a wooded area, and they have trails all over the place and 4000 acres." Taking a break from running to enjoy other physical activities like backpacking or hiking has been a part of Bill's lifestyle. For example, he will go for a four or five-day canoeing and camping trip in the Adirondacks or a three-day bike trip to Vermont. Bill cites being blessed as most important of all: "Like I say, I'm pretty spiritual, and I just think God must be watching over me, I believe."

A few words of wisdom from Bill:

An ultramarathon is like going through life itself. You have your ups and downs. You're going pretty well, you're feeling good, you're euphoric, and then things start going bad. You get depressed a little bit. Sometimes you sit down alongside the road because you've had it, you think you're done. . . . What I've seen with people is when they thought they were done, they would pick themselves up and get going. And that's what you have to do. Keep picking yourself up. It's hard sometimes, but I think you've got to get yourself up and keep moving.

Shirley Pettijohn, 2015

Shirley Pettijohn, 83
Faced Discrimination as a Woman Runner

SHIRLEY WAS OUT RUNNING before Title 1X, before women were accepted as equals in sports, or accepted at all in the sport of running. Here, in her words, is an example of what she was confronted with:

> I was about five to six miles into my run, which was going to be about 12 miles. And a neighbor parked his car on the curb, and he was going into the drug store there, and I happened to be coming along at the same time, and he said, "What are you doing?" I said, "I'm running." He said, "Get in my car and I'll take you home. . . ." They were naysayers, and they weren't open to the possibilities, especially for women.

Back in the 1970s when Shirley started running, the veil of discrimination had not yet been lifted, and women were routinely ridiculed for participating in road racing. She reminded me how Kathy Switzer had been physically assaulted in the Boston Marathon by the director of the race simply because she was a woman, before the gender barrier had been broken. Shirley sums up how she and other women were treated in those early years:

> Back then, those of my age will recall that women who ran were snickered at, looked down on; comments were made to their face. And so I ran around and around the outside of the house, and in

cold weather I ran around and around inside the house. And at that time I was not the only female that was running in the closet, shall we say. There were women who would go out after dark and run in their neighborhood when their neighbors couldn't see them.

Shirley Pettijohn was born on December 22, 1933, in Halls, Mo. She married her high-school sweetheart at 19, adopted two children, and worked as a secretary. Shirley's running career has spanned nearly four decades, and she has competed in approximately 900 races. Although her running resume includes 14 marathons, nine of which are New York City Marathons with a personal best time in 4:17 at age 59, Shirley presently limits her events from the 5K to the five-miler. I had a chance to catch up with her at the New Jersey Cross-Country 8K Championships in October of 2016, where she captured first place in her age group. In recent years, Shirley relishes her weekend races, and refreshments that follow, with her teammates, Melva, Diane, Pat, and Caroline, on the only 80s women's running team from New Jersey.

Keys to Shirley's Success, health, and Longevity

Shirley stresses the importance of perseverance as a key and says, "That's what I was exposed to in my family, you just keep going. You don't lay down and quit." She further believes that her cross-training, which included biking, strength building, and lots of stretching, has enhanced her efforts over the years.

In closing, Shirley shared this: "Follow your dream. If running doesn't work for you, go do what works for you, like bowling, horseback riding, but try to keep active."

George Hirsch, 82
Longtime Publisher of
Runner's World

Current Chairman of NYRR

Being a founder of the all-five-borough New York City Marathon, George had a special place in his heart for this world-renowned race. At 75 years of age he was going to give it a final try. But first, he was off to the Windy City and the Chicago Marathon. George entered this prestigious event, and intended to use the race as a tune-up for New York. His plan was to do a long training run of perhaps 10 to 15 miles and then pull off the course. Well, that's not exactly what happened. George explains: "I couldn't get off the course. I couldn't get a cab. I asked a police officer, 'What's the best way to get a cab?' And he says, 'You're not going to get a cab.' So I kept running and finished. . . . So I ran 3:58." George broke the four-hour barrier at age 75 and won his age group.

Just a few weeks after running in Chicago, George competed in his last of 40 marathons in New York. He provides the commentary:

> Then, I ran New York, and I ran with friends of mine. For six or seven miles, a friend of mine named Germán Silva (who won NYC Marathon twice) ran it with me. And then Amby (Burfoot, Boston winner of '68) met me and he stayed with me. And then Bill (Rodgers, four-time winner of NYC and Boston) picked us up over

George Hirsch, 2017

on 1st Avenue, so maybe there were six miles to go. And I was having a terrible day. It was awful. I didn't run well. I had to walk a bunch of times. But it was my final marathon, so Amby and Bill and I finished together. . . . I won my age group in 4:06.

George Meets Joan

In the Boston Marathon of 1979, George met a woman named Sue at the start line, and, after the gun went off, another woman, Joan, came up alongside the two of them, and they all introduced themselves and ran together. George takes it from there:

> The great American woman runner then was Patti Lyons (known today as Patti Catalano). She was the top American marathon runner and she was somewhere out ahead of us. After about 10 miles or so, Sue dropped back. . . . And then the crowd was shouting, "Second woman, second woman." Joan was second at that point to Patti Lyons, who was a good friend of mine. About mile 16, into the hills, Joanie starts moving ahead of me after running together for almost two hours. I was running over my head. I shouldn't even be there, right? I'm a 44-year-old guy, you know. Then Sue comes up alongside me, so I start running with her. And then we hear Joanie has just passed Patti. So Sue and I finished together, and there was Joanie, and she had the wreath on. She had beaten Patty. . . . I ran 2:38. That was my best marathon time, and one of my best times in terms of enjoyment and making friends that stay friends.

(This victory at the Boston Marathon kicked off Joan Benoit Samuelson's brilliant running career and put her on the world stage. She won Boston again in 1983, triumphed in the first woman's Olympic marathon with the gold medal in Los Angeles a year later, and set the woman's American record at the 1985 Chicago Marathon, which stood for 18 years.)

Work and Running Intertwine

George Hirsch was born on June 21, 1934, in Manhattan and grew up in New Rochelle, N.Y. In his childhood, he notes, "I was a terrible athlete, but I loved sports." He ran track in high school and college, but says he was mediocre. After graduating from Princeton in 1956, he went into the military and became a naval officer on a ship stationed in Naples, Italy, for three years. Back home, he went to Harvard Business School, received a MBA degree, and began his career at Time-Life International, spending five years there from 1962 to 1967. During this time, he married Brenda, and they had two sons. Striking out on his own, he left his job at Time, Inc. to start *New York Magazine.*

In late 1968, soon after launching his magazine, George began running again for the first time in 10 years. A couple of friends persuaded George to run the Boston Marathon, which he completed in a swift time of 3:26. It was his first race since running the half mile in college.

Around this time, George also started his own running magazine entitled, *The Runner.* Yet, a deal was struck with Rodale Press to have George head the magazine, *Runner's World,* and merge their two publications. Thus, for the next two decades, George published the lead running magazine in the country. And he had the best of both worlds: "When I was doing *Runners World,* my day job was good because everyone could go out and run at lunch." George was running and racing at the time he was publishing *Runner's World,* integrating his work with his passion for the sport.

Besides his publishing work at *New York Magazine, Runner's World,* and *Men's Health Magazine,* George worked with NBC TV doing commentary for distance running events, like the 5000 and 10,000 meters and the marathon, at three different Olympic Games—Los Angeles in 1984, Seoul in 1988, and Barcelona in 1992. While preparing for the Seoul Olympics, George had gone to the U.S. Olympic trials in New Jersey to get acquainted with the runners. He had run 10 miles with his friend Frank Shorter, a former gold medal Olympian, the day before the trials and had no intention of running in the race. Later that day he met a charming woman, Shay, at the expo, and hoped to catch up with her the next day before the start of the race. In the morning at the start line, however, Shay was nowhere in sight, so George began to run in the race to look for her. Finally, about five miles into the New Jersey Waterfront Marathon, he found her. George hadn't run a marathon in four years, but running and talking with Shay summoned up the fire and determination he needed to complete the entire 26.2 miles. A year later they were married at the Boat House Café in Central Park.

The Onward Shay Boise Marathon

For a quarter century George loved and cherished Shay until her passing three years ago. Her 11-year battle with cancer, which included two stem-cell transplants, was over. There were two women that originated a marathon in Boise, Idaho, to honor Shay and her positive attitude throughout her struggles with cancer. Shay had signed her blog, "Onward Shay," so the marathon was named The Onward Shay Boise Marathon. The inaugural race took place on October 30, 2016, as George recalls:

> They had a relay as well. So Bill (Rodgers) ran the first leg of the relay, Frank (Shorter) ran the first leg, Joanie (Benoit Samuelson) ran the first leg, I ran one, Amby (Burfoot) ran it, Mary Wittenberg, who used to head the New York Marathon, she did it. We all went out and spent the weekend. And the local brewery came out with Onward Shay Ruby Red Pale Ale, and it was in all the stores and pubs for the month of October. . . . Joanie left us all in the dust. You have to know, it doesn't matter how old you are, how many injuries you got, how slow you are, people stay competitive. They want to beat each other. . . . And we had a bandit runner. A bandit is someone who runs without a number. So in the Onward Shay, we didn't know it until after, we had a bandit runner—Tom Hanks.

At 82, George is one of the fastest age-group competitors in the New York City region and, indeed, the country, and still runs about one race a month. In his last 10 of 40 marathons he has won his age group, and at the Bronx 5K in September of 2016, George ran a sizzling 26:57, at an 8:42/mile pace. That is phenomenal! Okay, George, what are your secrets?

Keys to George's Success, Health, and Longevity

George believes that keeping active, both mentally and physically,

161

has enhanced his vitality and well-being: "I would say, whether it's your mind or your body, keep moving, keep engaged, keep learning." George also feels that running has been essential: "I'm one of the really lucky people who's gotten the benefits of running—the health benefits, the social benefits, the friendships, the community. And I've also earned a living at it." Lastly, he adds:

> I think a big test for all of us is not how well we handle our successes, it's how well we manage our adversity. And that to me is a bigger test. You go through personal problems, professional problems, and I think it tests your resilience, the sense of your character and who you are. The worst thing for me was when Shay was in the hospital for 100 days. . . . But you keep going forward, and here I am.

In conclusion, George shared this: "Never make the big decision on the uphill. No one gets the tailwind the whole way. There are potholes you have to navigate and things you have to get through, so don't make big decisions when you're in a difficult spot. Wait until you're at least on level ground."

Joe Handelman, 86
At 80 Ran an Ultra-Marathon

AT A 5K RACE IN THE DEAD OF WINTER, here's what Joe said he and his running buddies did:

> It was five below zero and so cold they wouldn't let the race go on. When I notified my wife that the race had been cancelled, she said it was a very sensible thing to do. So when I get home my wife says, "Since they called off the race, why were you so late?" I said, "Because my friends and I ran the race twice."

Joe's wife wasn't too pleased with that reply. She often thought he was overdoing it.

Joe Handelman was born on April 22, 1930, in New Rochelle, N.Y. In high school Joe was the captain of his cross-country team, and also ran on the track team with Lou Jones, a gold-medal winner at the Melbourne Olympics in 1956. In his senior year Joe took on the young upstart. He states, "In the first race I beat Lou. I kept him on the outside of the track the whole way. I never beat him again, but we stayed friends all our lives until he died about four years ago."

After being on the cross-county team and graduating from Princeton University, Joe took a break from running for the next 15 years to complete his military service in Fairbanks, Alaska; marry Susan and have two sons, Cary and Jeffrey, and a daughter, Leslie; receive his MBA from New York University; and enter the family business as an investment advisor. In the process he gained about 50

Joe Handelman, 2016

pounds and became overweight and out of shape. However, in his late 30s, stirred to action by President Kennedy's emphasis on fitness, Joe began jogging up to three miles six days a week, and within five years his devotion to running and racing was solidified. When living in New Rochelle and working on Wall Street in his 50s, Joe was training 50 to 70 miles a week. He says, "I ran from 5:30 to 7:00 in the morning. Then, three to four times a week I ran from 10:00 to 12:00 at night after the kids went to sleep." Now this is serious training, and his personal records reflect this dedication. In his early 50s, he ran a 5K in 18:56, a 10K in 39:30, and the Jersey Shore Marathon in 3:17. Overall, Joe reports completing 1311 races, including about 30 marathons and 14 ultra-marathons. He remarks, "My mileage is in excess of 60,000 miles, and I am on my third trip around the world."

The competitive spirit was the driving force behind Joe's passion for the sport of road racing:

> I ran like someone was chasing me with a bayonet and I had to get away from them. I wanted to beat the other guys in my age group, and I was fanatical about the competition. I made so much noise they thought I was dying. One time, I was in a race moaning and groaning, and the guy in front of me turns around and asks me if I was alright, and I passed him at the end that way.

Later in life Joe began his incredible ultra-marathon journey. He ran the Sybil Ludington 50K Run, a 32-mile race, annually from age 64 to 80, only missing two years with hamstring issues. For a time, he held the course record for 70 and older, and believes he is the only 80-year-old to have completed the race. When Joe finished his final ultra-marathon two days after his 80th birthday, the organizers brought out a cake, and everyone sang happy birthday and celebrated the occasion. Unfortunately, within a month Joe was stricken with meningitis and, shortly after, suffered a stroke. His son, Cary, says: "He was on a respirator and unconscious for a few days. We really feared he would not regain consciousness." But Joe showed his tenacity, rebounded out of the coma, and spent several months in a rehab facility to regain the ability to talk and walk with the aid of a walker. Joe says, "I miss the running more than anything." Since his father's stroke, however, Cary has taken up running in his 50s, and Joe goes to his son's races and gets to see some of the old gang. In this vicarious way Joe stays connected to the sport he has so loved, and it has helped to soften the sadness that he feels.

Keys to Joe's Success, Health, and Longevity

Joe notes, "We had heart problems in the family. Both my brothers had heart attacks and bypasses, so I always wanted to save my heart. It was a big reason to run for me. . . . Running has saved my life."

Joe adds, "My whole life has revolved around running. My health, my mental health, my personal and social life."

Erika Abraham, 78
The Proposal at the Finish Line

Back in 1988, it was a night of fun and frolicking in Central Park at the annual New Year's Eve five-mile run put on by the New York Road Runners club, with plenty of champagne along the course. Erika and her boyfriend, Roy, joined in the festive occasion. As Erika reminisces:

> It was the Midnight Run, and Roy and I decided to go with a group of friends and rent a limousine and do the run and celebrate the New Year. They had firecrackers and fireworks going off, and I remember tables of champagne throughout the run. Well, there's more to it. Roy proposed at the finish line. He says, "Will you marry me?" I'm thinking he was on a runner's high or high on champagne, and I said, "Are you serious?". . . . On the way home in the limousine we were with our friends. And then, of course, the two of us knew I'd said, "Yes," and we were both giddy and happy.

Erika and Roy were married in October of 1989, about nine months after the wedding proposal at the Midnight Run finish line. This was Erika's second go-around and a vast improvement over her first marriage.

Running to the Rescue

Erika Abraham was born on May 22, 1938, in White Plains, N.Y., two months premature. She had this to say about her birth:

Erika Abraham, 2015

I am one of a set of premature twins, so I learned early on that I had to survive because my sister and I were seven-month babies. I was four pounds, four ounces, and she was three pounds, 11 ounces. We both survived. I think that's where the will to survive began for me and, yes, my twin sister is still alive.

Around 1970, when she was in her early 30s, Erika's first husband left her and their three children, ages three, seven, and nine, to fend for themselves. Suddenly, Erika became a single parent, raising her kids on her own with little money or education. After countless years fraught with low self-esteem and isolation, she finally found a fulfilling life passion and a resource to rely on—running.

Erika began running back in 1983 when she was 45. Looking back, she recalls:

My youngest son, Greg, liked to run. He didn't like to be seen running with me because I was not color coordinated in my attire, I kid you not, so we ran in the fields on the hills. He was a difficult child to raise, and that was his way of running off steam, but he was a pain in the neck, and I wanted to keep tabs on him, and he challenged me to run. And that got me moving, it got me loving something. . . . I was in Binghamton (New York), and I was working two jobs, and it was hard money-wise. I don't want to dwell on the past, but it also leads to why I am motivated to run and to succeed. The children's father, my husband, left me with three children and eventually no money. That's history that hurt me tremendously, to the point that I realized that no matter what else I did in life, nothing would ever, ever, affect me so negatively.

When asked what inspired her to run, Erika spoke from the heart:

I did not have much confidence in who I was. I did not like myself. I went to school, I went to work, I raised the kids. I drank so much caffeine that I was bouncing off the walls and doorframes, and I think basically it was a feeling of not having self-worth. . . . But the more I ran the better I felt. It was about succeeding. I was a good student and a good worker, and I got a good job. None of that meant anything, because I was a lonely person and it was a lonely life. But once I got out running, it gave me wolf-whistles. The guys gave me wolf-whistles. It made me feel, well, maybe I was a good person, a special person, maybe I was a pretty person, maybe I was a good runner, and it gave me self-confidence to go out and try different things. I no longer had the fear of trying something new. Remember, the divorce devastated me. I was a nobody. I was not accepted with our friends anymore because I was the fifth wheel on the wagon. I was a threat to the wives, so I wasn't invited there anymore. I was cut off socially. Divorce was not recognized at that time. I could not get a credit card in my name. I had no confidence to do anything after he walked out. So I had to have the strength to fight and finally find out where I belonged in the world. . . . Then I found out I could succeed in running. And I ran races, I won awards, I won money, I felt really good.

After moving from Binghamton to Spring Valley, N.Y., in 1985, Erika was challenged by a co-worker to a run on April 1, 1986, (no joke). She took her friend up on it, and she considers this the inception of her running and racing career. Erika was 48, and she plunged right into her training and attending races. Within a year and a half, Erika was registered for her first New York City Marathon, although she had a host of doubters and disbelievers. However, she got the best of her skeptics:

When I was working in the lab, believe it or not, people bet money on how many miles of the marathon I would do. My co-workers didn't think I would finish. My youngest son even made a bet. Well, I got enough money after I'd finished the race to buy a good pair of running shoes.

39 Marathons and 11 Ultra-Marathons

Over the past three decades, Erika has completed approximately 700 races, averaging 20 to 25 competitions a year from the 5K to the ultra-marathon. In her mid-50s, she was in peak form and set all of her personal best times, including her best 5K and 10K in just over 7:00/mile pace, and her 10-miler at 7:40/mile. Yet, her favorite distance was the marathon and ultra-marathon, with her best time in the marathon at the Duchess County Classic in New York when she was 55. She ran it in 3:37. Erika has completed five Boston Marathons, six New York City Marathons, the Country Music Marathon in Nashville and the Adirondack Marathon several times each, as well as many others. But one of her all-time favorite races was a 60K ultra- marathon, running 37.3 miles in the pouring rain while traversing six loops around Central Park in New York City at age 54 in a time of 6:22.

Then there were the fun runs, as Erika calls them, like the Mt. Washington Road Race, a 7.6 mile run with the motto "Only One Hill," and the Whiteface Mountain Uphill Foot Race, an 8.2 mile run up the mountainside with loads of switchbacks, where Erika placed first in her age group all four years she ran the race. These are exceedingly strenuous events, and Erika says, "You've got to try something like that, you've got to do something nutty. Sometimes you have to meet something head on and challenge yourself just to see how far you can go, because you never know what you can do until you try."

For Erika, running has had a very special meaning in her life. She wrote the following in an article which attempts to capture that essence:

> Instead of watching the world go by I became a part of that world. I became involved in something bigger and better than I ever imagined. . . . It meant meeting other new runners and making many new friends. It meant getting out of my shell. Being less reserved and quiet and smiling a whole lot more. It meant not feeling so alone in a world where, as a single working parent with three sons, I did not easily or comfortably fit in. . . . It meant having fun in life. As time went on, I also joined running clubs, expanded my friendships, volunteered at some races, and started to write articles about running. . . . The confidence gained was immeasurable. The friendships formed were unlimited, and I became the person that I believe I was meant to be.

Erika believes she can be an inspiration to others:

Particularly as an older runner, hopefully I can inspire somebody else that's older to get out of the rocking chair, discard the rocking-chair image for older people, and try something—even if it's not running. It could be walking. It may just be another sport. But just to get them out there and be active.

Training for Erika meant going out on runs, with little cross-training or speed work. The first 10 years she began running every day, 5 to 10 miles a day, 40 to 50 miles a week, but as she got older, she tapered down to five days a week and cut back her mileage accordingly. And Erika has always relished running on her own, being in touch with nature and the peace and solitude within herself. She vividly describes what it was like on those training runs:

> I want to talk to the birds. I want to talk to the squirrels. I want to talk to myself. And then I talk to my deceased parents. And no one can hear me when I talk to myself, and they can't think that I'm crazy. This is my peace, John. This is my alone time. Years ago, because of the schedule that I had, the only time I had to myself was when I was able to go out on the road, the only peace I had to go into my own head, the only time I would let nobody come in. Nobody would bother me. No phones, no deadlines, no overtime, no kids.

Tenacity of Spirit

Injuries are always a concern for runners, and Erika is no exception. Her first major injury, however, came from falling off her bike while training for her second triathlon, not from running. Swerving to avoid a car that had pulled out in front of her, she went head first over the bike, landing in a ditch on the side of the road, and was temporarily knocked out. Although she suffered from nerve damage to her cheek, which needed prompt surgical repair, and bones broken in her shoulder, Erika did not let that deter her. As she explains, "But I did a race two and a half weeks later, a 5K, and I think I did a 23-minute something. My arm was in a sling, and I was high on Tylenol and codeine, and I still came in second in my age group."

The expression Erika uses to characterize herself is "tenacity of spirit." Take, for example, the time she was training for the Inaugural Country Music Marathon and slipped on snow-covered ice and fell and broke her wrist. She was put into a full arm cast and wondered if she should continue her training. "I asked my orthopedic surgeon, 'Can I run?' And he said, 'Erika, if you run, just don't fall.'" So she trained for the marathon for the next four weeks with the cast on, and by the time of the race the cast had been removed, and she remembers coming in third in her age group.

Then about six years ago at age 72, Erika fell after a mile into a 5K race in Chester, N.Y., injuring her right knee. It required arthroscopic surgery. Her doctor told her at the time not to run anymore, and this was her response:

> Obviously, I disobeyed him and didn't listen to him. He told me again a year ago, no more running, when the other knee was done. He said, "Erika, you know what's going to happen, no more running . . ." Well, I'm hanging in there, because they say when you come to the end of your rope tie a knot and hang on. And that's what I did.

She did make a concession to the doctor to go slower and shorter distances, but Erika remains a runner and competitor to this day—a testament to her tenacity of spirit.

Keys to Erika's Success, Health, and Longevity

Erika lists several keys as important: "My love of running, being goal-oriented, being challenged, my desire to succeed, having my name in print, and the surgical skill of my orthopedic surgeon on both knees to keep me running." She acknowledges that all the long-distance training for marathons and ultra-marathons probably had a negative impact on her knees, but says otherwise she wouldn't have gotten the same enjoyment out of running. Family support also appears to be a prominent factor. Roy has attended nearly all of Erika's races and has competed in many of them himself, and her three sons have encouraged and affirmed her love of running, while each son has done some of his own running and racing. Erika proudly proclaims that none of the boys have been able to eclipse any of her best times in races and she doesn't expect them to do so in the future.

There are two other considerations that Erika elaborates on. She says:

> One of the keys is probably because I'm a tough old bird. I can get knocked down, but I can get right back up again. I was bullied as a kid. I went through a lot of uncomfortable situations in life. . . . And I go back to the fact that I was a preemie-baby when I was born, so I was tough from day one.

Lastly, Erika believes her success and longevity in the sport of running can be partly attributed to this: "It's following through on something. It's not only going to the starting line of whatever you want to do. It's actually following through, not dropping out in midstream."

Toward the end of the interview Erika shared this: "I want to read a quote I like from Nelson Mandela. It says, 'Do not judge me by my successes. Judge me by how many times I fell down and got back up again.'"

Finally, a few enlightening words from Erika: "Regardless of what you are thrown in life, when life throws you a curve ball, turn it into a home run."

Geoff Etherington, 88

One of the Fastest Men His Age in America

GEOFF SENT IN HIS $5 ENTRY FEE for the Inaugural Chicago Marathon, better known at the time as the Mayor Daley Marathon. But at 50 years of age, Geoff had only been in two previous races, a 5-miler and 10-miler. Well, the race was a lot harder than Geoff expected, and he admits, "I overdid it. I couldn't walk and had to get crutches so I could manage to fly home." Yet, considering the lack of sufficient training, running a 3:38 for his first marathon foreshadowed what was to come.

Geoff Etherington was born on December 21, 1928, in London, England. Soon after his birth, the family returned to the town above the Arctic Circle in Russia where his father was employed. However, with little sunshine or available fresh produce, Geoff had acquired rickets and scurvy as a toddler. Around this time, he and his family moved to Milwaukee, Wis., where he quickly recovered from his illnesses. Geoff's first attempt at running came in high school, when he and some other runners created their own cross-country team. Soon after graduation he enlisted and served in the army of occupation in Korea for a year before the onset of the Korean War. He then returned to continue his education. Geoff's college credentials are impressive and include a mechanical engineering degree from Purdue, an MBA from Northwestern, a law degree from Loyola of

Geoff Etherington, 2016

Chicago, and an MD degree from Yale. Geoff primarily worked in management, and eventually secured ownership of companies that manufactured automotive parts. For 25 years he also headed a facility affiliated with Yale that specialized in physiology research. Geoff has five children from previous marriages and has been married to Marie for the past quarter century.

In his early 40s Geoff returned to running. He was overweight and began to follow the Canadian Airforce plan of fitness by jogging a mile and building up to two miles about five days a week. It wasn't until he was 50 that he started running seriously and training for races, but by his mid-50s, Geoff was scorching the racing circuit. Take a look at these swift times: A fall marathon in Boston in 2:44, at 6:17/mile, and a 5K in 16:56, at 5:27/mile. And at age 60 he ran the New Haven National Championship 20K, a 12.4 mile race, in a blistering 1:13, at 5:56/mile, a course record in his age group at the time.

Running between 20 and 30 races a year from age 50 to 84, Geoff thinks he has competed in nearly 1000 races. In his early 80s he was just about unbeatable as a masters competitor. For instance, at 84 in a race in Plainville, Conn., he ran a 5K in slightly over 24 minutes, in an 8:00/mile pace. According to Geoff, "The *Running Times* (Magazine) had ranked me first in the nation when I was 82 and 83, in the over 80s." But soon after that Plainville 5K, Geoff had a second arthroscopic surgery on his right knee that slowed him down considerably, and he lost his competitive edge. By the time I had met with Geoff for this interview in the summer of 2016, however, he was making his comeback at 87 and had recently run the 5K Docs Race in Orange, Conn., in 29:48, at 9:36/mile. No doubt, Geoff is one of the fastest 88-year-old runners in the United States.

Keys to Geoff's Success, Health, and Longevity

Geoff believes a basic key to his robust constitution is inheritance. "Part of it has to be genetics," he says. "My parents both died in their 90s. My mother died at 90 and my father at 94, and they didn't die a natural death either. They committed suicide together." Geoff has this to say about diet: "If you eat too much and the wrong kind of food, you'll get obese. If you eat a lot of saturated fats you tend to get cardiac problems." Geoff eats more fish and poultry than meat, likes fruits and vegetables, and also says, "I usually have a drink with dinner every night, either wine or beer."

Some guidance from Geoff:

> My advice would be don't smoke, don't eat saturated fats, and find some form of exercise, any exercise you can do and you like. My wife would never run. I can't even get her to go out and walk. But she'll play tennis five times a week, because she's very competitive and likes to be hitting something, like hitting the ball. I'd rather her be hitting the ball than me, you know.

Bill Rodgers, 69
An American Living Legend

O<small>FF ON A RUN WITH HIS BUDDIES</small>, Bill faces the beast:

I was training with my teammates through the western suburbs, not too far from here. They were some of the top guys in the world, the top Americans. And we were running along doing a 20-miler and Alberto Salazar is with us. He's a senior in high school and was one of the best high-school kids in the county. He could run with us, you know, and he'd do 15 miles with us. But it's pretty hard for an 18-year-old kid to stay with us 28-year-olds who are pushing it. We were stronger than he was at the time, but he was coming up. Anyway, he's kind of in back of us a little, and we were running a good pace. And out of the corner of my eye I see this huge Great Dane running at us, charging our group. Probably weighed as much as Alberto, it was a big dog. And the dog comes up and circles around confronting Alberto, like it was going to jump him, and I thought he was going to be attacked. So I ran up, you know, he's a teammate and a friend, and I threw my keys and I hit the dog. I didn't hurt it, but I scared it, and the dog takes off and runs away. And I grabbed my keys and we're out of there.

The Growing Pains

As many of us know, Bill Rodgers is thought of as the most successful American marathoner of all time, or at least shares the pedestal with

Bill Rodgers, 2016

the renowned Frank Shorter. But Bill had his growing pains on the way up. Take, for example, his first attempt at the Boston Marathon in 1973. Bill describes what happened:

> I automatically thought I'd do well, but the marathon can be a very cruel event. Well, it was terrible. It was the heat, and I didn't know how to pace myself, and there wasn't adequate water on the course. I staggered with cramps in my hamstrings and my legs. I made it to the top of Heartbreak Hill, but I could look over and about two miles away was Jamaica Plain where I lived, and I kind of jogged and walked home. You know, I had my tail between my legs, and I'd gotten beaten up, slapped in the face. I quit running for three months. I thought this was a terrible, terrible sport.

After the disaster of that first Boston Marathon, Bill determined he needed to move to a warmer climate to train adequately in the winter. He and his wife, Ellen, set out for California, but within a few months they were drawn back to the East, settling for a short stint in Virginia before landing right back where they'd started, in the greater Boston area. Up next for Bill was only his second marathon, the Bay State Marathon, where he redeemed himself with a win in a rather small field of 70 runners. He says, "I then had my PR (personal record) and was no longer a dropout." But for Bill that race was just a warm up for the big one, his second attempt at Boston in 1974. Yet, act two was nearly a replication of the first. Bill ran with the lead pack for the first 19 miles, but, once again, Heartbreak Hill proved to be his downfall, and he stopped with severe leg cramping and contemplated quitting the race. But a fellow runner encouraged Bill to continue, and the cramps subsided enough for him to finish in 14th place with a new PR in 2:19.

The New York City Marathon was on the horizon in 1974. This time Bill felt well prepared. A month earlier he'd flattened the field of 445 runners at the prestigious seven-mile, Falmouth Road Race, easily outdueling America's finest miler, Marty Liquori, and coasting to victory. And his training was solid and on target, running 100 miles a week leading up to New York. Here is Bill's take on the race:

New York was four laps of Central Park and extremely hilly. I took off with the gun because I wanted to win first prize and go to Greece. I wanted to see where the first sports of the world were and what the Olympics was all about. I was way, way ahead in the lead at 21 miles, and I should have won. If it had been cooler weather, I could have won, but I didn't run smart. It was held in September, and it was 90-95 degrees and very, very hot, just brutal. I should have stayed back. If I'd stayed back with the other runners I think I would have won. So I went to the side of the road with cramps in my legs again, and I ended up in fifth place.

Bill Rodgers was born on December 23, 1947, in Hartford, Conn. The family moved to Newington, Conn., when Bill was seven, and he remained there until he went off to college. He believes that being active as a child in the Cub Scouts, Boy Scouts, riding his bike, and always being outside, helped him develop his skills. After running an impressive mile in gym class and being written up in the local paper for his feat, Bill joined the high-school cross-country team and its inspirational coach, Frank O'Rourke. Bill notes, "In the winters we would run indoors in the school hallways, because we didn't have a track." His friend Jason and brother Charlie were also a part of the running teams, and Bill point out, "We all cheered for each other. Track and cross-country are team sports, so you cheer for your teammates. You know, you have to have that fun, that camaraderie. Most people never get chosen to be on a team in high school. Our sports system in America, unfortunately, and probably for many, many nations, is for the few." The U.S. President was also an inspirational figure for Bill, who states:

It was the era of John F. Kennedy, and physical fitness was being discussed. I remember to this day when President Kennedy was killed. I went outside and I ran a mile and I tried to break a five-minute mile. I think I ran like 5:01. You know, he had a big impact on me and, in fact, on all Americans.

By his senior year in high school, Bill had moved up to third in the state rankings in the two-mile race and was running the mile around 4:29. He says, "In my senior year, I think I won every cross-country meet I was in, except maybe one or two." He considered himself a solid high-school runner but not a national runner. Before going off to college, Bill's parents had their concerns about his running and where it was taking him, since the sport at that time was not well understood. As Bill thinks back:

> I remember my parents saying to me, "Bill, are you sure you want to keep running?" My parents were from the World War Two generation. There's no leisure time to go for a run, they were at work. My Dad was the head of the Mechanical Engineering Department at Connecticut, and my mother was a nurse's aide and had four children.

But Bill was undeterred. At a major state competition which he won, he met Amby Burfoot, winner of the Boston Marathon of 1968, who swayed Bill to attend Wesleyan University and join their cross-country team. The two of them became buddies, teammates, and in Bill's sophomore year, roommates and running partners. Amby and another teammate, Jeff Galloway, who became an Olympian in 1972, provide Bill with key mentorship to hone his running skills in those initial years at Wesleyan. Bill remarks, "So I had this entry into the world of running with two guys who were very focused on excelling, but also loved the beauty of the sport and understood the sport. I had these two great teachers. I was real lucky."

Amby was preparing for the Boston Marathon. Bill recalls:

> So Amby had this dream, and I was training with him. He would play this song, "To Dream the Impossible Dream," and I would play the record too. . . So we trained together, and he taught me about trail running. Run on dirt and grass as much as you can. And today, 40 years later, all the coaches are having the runners do that.

By his senior year at Wesleyan, Bill's life, and the country in general, were in turmoil. Bill remarks:

> The Vietnam War was raging, and I was very against our involvement in that war. So I was inducted and took the physical, but I got conscientious objector status along with my brother Charlie and

183

Jason. But it was chaos, America was in chaos. So I didn't know where I was going or what was going to happen.

Just after setting his PR in the indoor two-miler in 8:58, Bill quit running in the winter of 1969 in his senior year. He says, "Everything fell apart. The student strike came and shut the school down. I didn't know what was going on in my life anymore." Around this time, Bill started smoking cigarettes.

To fulfill his conscientious objector requirement for community service, Bill took a position at a hospital as an orderly. The job was reasonably satisfying, but after a year and a half, Bill and another worker got the boot after attempting some labor organizing for better pay. By this time, he had married Ellen, who provided needed financial support for the next year, until Bill could find another job and get back on his feet. He laments, "I was sick of doing nothing. And with the smoking, I started wheezing a lot." He and his friend Jason then went to see the Boston Marathon. Bill reminisces:

> I saw Amby Burfoot and Jeff Galloway, and they were right up there near the front. . . . All these things must have come together in mind. That's when I joined the Y and ran on the indoor track, a 160 meter, little, rinky-dink track. I was making my move to return to running. Losing my job, having my motorcycle stolen, they were blessings. The circumstances allowed me to get back to what I was best at, which was my running, and find what I could do with it.

Bill began to train where he and Ellen lived in Jamaica Plain, running laps around a picturesque pond and its surrounding natural beauty. He then met Jock Semple, the director of the Boston Marathon, and joined the BAA (Boston Athletic Association), and his running took off. Bill remarks, "I started training twice a day and moved up to 100 miles a week. Train, train, train, that was my life, you know. I was like a full-time runner then." By this time Bill had given up cigarettes, and his sights were set on the Boston Marathon of 1973. But running back then had its drawbacks, as Bill explains:

> I remember those early days. We'd be yelled at a lot. People would be driving by in cars and asking, "What are you running

for?" They would yell out, "Get a job." Even some of my relatives asked me, "Why are you running? You're not going to make any money at it." And they were right, in the beginning I didn't make any money at it.

Of course, eventually Bill did quite well for himself financially.

Reaching the Next Level

After Bill's disappointing performances in his first two Boston Marathons and first New York City Marathon, the course of events were about to change. Soon after the New York debacle of '74, Bill headed south to the Philadelphia Marathon where he claimed victory in 2:21, on a very cold and windy day. Acknowledging his win, Bill comments, "What I'm trying to do is make my comeback. I figured if I get beaten down, It's like Frank Sinatra said, you know, when you fall down you have to get back in the race, and that's what I did." Bill joined the Greater Boston Track Club and cemented a strong bond with his coach and teammates. He notes, "We had still one of America's greatest marathon coaches, Coach Billy Squires. And we had a whole slew of teammates all like me, people who ran in high school or college and wanted to stay active and explore, well, am I done? Well, maybe I'm not done."

The game-changer for Bill takes place in Morocco, as he discloses:

My breakthrough came in '75 in my third year of training. I ran the World Cross-Country Championships, which is like the Olympics of cross-country. There are 200 countries in the world, right? It's a big lineup. You're competing against everyone. The milers, the 5000 meter guys, the 10K guys, the marathoners. The whole world is there. But I didn't have my shoes, I forgot my shoes. So one of my teammates, Gary Tuttle, loaned me his shoes. . . . This was a 12 kilometer, seven and a half mile race, and I got into the lead with two other guys and we broke away. That's the first time I defeated Frank (Shorter), and I came in third and took bronze. So only four other American men have ever medaled in World Cross-Country, ever in the 100 years in cross-country. I was sky-high.

After his exceptional performance in Morocco, Bill headed to the Boston Marathon a month later. Here is how the race unfolded:

It was a beautiful day to run. At the six-mile mark I was up with the leaders, my friend Tom Fleming, Mario Guavas from Mexico, and a Canadian guy named Jerome Drayton. To this day, 41 years later, Jerome is still the Canadian record holder. And someone yelled, "Go Canada," because he had the Canadian Maple Leaf on. Well, someone is yelling, "Go Canada." To hell with that, and I took off. We were side by side, and I surged to change the pace, and he neglected to go with me. At 23 miles I see Jason, my old roommate, and he's on the course on a bike yelling out his support. . . . I was leading the Boston Marathon. John, it was like a dream. Jock Semple leaned out of the lead vehicle and said, "Bill, you're breaking the record." And when I won, my brother Charlie was at the finish line. . . . I ran the fastest time in the world that year in the race. 2:09:55 was the fourth-fastest time ever run, and I had the American record for six years. Suddenly I was a marathoner, and my life changed, and I got invitations to run other races around the world.

But as the saying goes, two steps forward and one back. Unfortunately for Bill, the step back was at the Olympics in Montreal of 1976, the only opportunity he had to compete at that level. In the U.S. trials, Bill and Frank Shorter had dominated in the marathon, but by the time of the Olympics Bill was not 100% and admits, "So I had a foot injury, and that was my undoing. I got crushed. It was another bad marathon that knocked me back. But I got a chance again to make a comeback." And, indeed, he did. Fred Lebow from the New York Road Runners club offered Bill a slot in the first all-five-borough New York City Marathon of 1976, and paid him a $3000 promotional fee to boot. Here is Bill's recollection of the race:

So Frank and I were going to duel again like in the Olympic Games and World Cross-Country Championships. It was a great challenge, but the tide had turned. So I went for it from the gun because this was my chance to get that redemption feeling, and Frank by then had his two Olympic medals. So by the half way mark I got away from Frank and a guy named Chris Stewart from Great Britain. I really pushed hard and got to the half in 1:03:57, so that's pretty quick. I knew I was going for the win, but I didn't know exactly where I was on the course. But when I got into Central Park, I love the park, it was like cross-country again. And I really sensed I'm going to take it, I'm going to win it, but I had no sense of my time, you know, until I finished. But then I saw I ran 2:10:10, my second-fastest time ever, and I think it was the second-best time in the world that year. . . . When I won New York, you know, I knew I'd come back.

At this time Bill's financial fortunes also made a dramatic improvement:

I started to race all over the world and make a living at it, and it was a good living. Prior to this, for two years I was a special-ed teacher, and I couldn't do both. I was trying to be the best in the world, and when you're up against the Russians, who are state-supported, the Finns who are state-supported, and runners around the world, and here we were trying to have our jobs at 40 hours a week. It was a challenge. So that's why we tried to change the sport to be professional, so we could train and compete full-time.

Back to the Boston Marathon in 1979, Bill went up against one of the world's best marathoners ever, Toshihiko Seko from Japan. Bill had beaten Seko in Japan's premier marathon at Fukuoka in 1977, but Seko had returned the favor a year later, out-battling Bill in 1978. Now, the classic duel shifted to Bill's home turf. He recalls the race:

Seko was highly touted in Japan as their top marathoner. And for the Japanese, they run honorably. It's not for the money, it's more for honor and representing your country. So it became a two-man race for about 18 miles, and he was hanging on me. Seko was a great strategy guy and a smart runner. He'd been running behind me, and sometimes he'd come up next to me. He was trying to see if I was getting tired, and then he'd make a move. But I'd beaten Seko before, so I thought, you know, maybe I could beat him again, and this is my course. I live here, I love the Boston course. But when he came to Boston, he didn't know the course. I got away on Heartbreak Hill, going up the hill. He didn't understand the hills were there. So when I pulled away, I pushed the pace and won the race. . . . Seko is ranked number two all-time as a marathoner and almost never lost. Shorter and I are tied for third and fourth, I think.

After the race Bill got a congratulatory phone call from the President and was invited to a State dinner at the White House. Bill reflects back:

Yah, I got a call from President Carter at our store in Boston. That was fantastic. I think he was the first president who was a runner. So Joan Benoit had won the women's division, and we went to the White House together. It was very nerve-wracking. I was scared, but it was a great, great honor.

Altogether, Bill has completed approximately 60 marathons and has been victorious in about 20 of them. He has run the Boston Marathon 17 times, winning his home-town race four times, and has entered nine New York City Marathons and triumphed in four of those. Bill declares, "By the time I turned 40, I'd run 50 hard marathons. We were running, trying to make a living, because we had to support ourselves, so we ran a lot of marathons. That's the way the sport was then, John." But Bill adds, "I had fun exploring the world and representing the United States. It meant so much to all of us to wear that American team insignia and compete against other countries in the world."

Into his 40s, Bill was still training by running over 100 miles a week and was still setting American age-group records. For instance, at age 40 he set the record in the 10K in 29:48, and held the 20K and half-marathon masters records as well. Bill also ran a 2:18 marathon at 40, and although not the record, it was still one of the fastest times ever run by an American at that age. Into his 50s and 60s, Bill has continued to excel, usually winning races in his age group. Taking into account that Bill had quit the sport for a year or two after college, he estimates he ran in 25 to 30 races a year since age 15, and completed 1500 events over the course of his career. Bill proudly asserts,

"I've run around 180,000 to 190,000 miles in my life. Like here to the moon almost. I'm trying to get to the moon."

Bill shares with us some of the hardships and happiness later in his life here:

> Well, at 55, I broke my leg and everything changed. Not only that, I had gotten married, and I had two daughters, and I got divorced. And this was hard. . . . What I'm saying, John, is that none of us live in a vacuum. We have our jobs and our family life and our friends and everything, and so that divorce was really, really hard, mentally and emotionally, for me. Then I was hit with prostate cancer. I was diagnosed in December, when I was 59 years old, and in January, a month later, I had radical surgery. I was 60 and that knocked me back. They had to watch the cancer, you know, because it started to come back, so I had to do radiation a year later. So I was knocked back again. But what also changed for me then was that I met another woman, Karen, who's my girlfriend now. She was a cancer patient too. She had breast cancer. Her cancer specialist said, "Why don't you try running?" And she did and she loved it. So we're runners together today. She beats me a lot. Holy cow, I can't catch her, you know.

Keys to Bill's Success, Health, and Longevity

Bill credits all the help he has received along the way for sustaining him in his road racing career. He sums it up here:

> I had a lot of support. I had good friends, my family, brother Charlie. Gail helped me a lot, so did Ellen, Karen does now. I had smart coaches. Coach O'Rourke, Coach Swanson, Coach Squires. Amby took me out to the trails, Galloway too. But also the race directors, the media people I met over the years. I had a big, close family. My mother and father, they supported us. They didn't totally understand it, but nobody did then.

Another factor for Bill is his motivation to keep his career going:

> I run almost every day, five to six days a week still. And I'll usually

189

run six miles a day, 40 miles a week, at almost 70. But this is my job, too, you have to remember, John. I'm still a runner, and I go to races and do promotional work at races. So I still make my living through the sport. I've been very lucky in that way.

Bill believes that changing his diet may also be a key, as he indicates here:

I learned a lot about eating a healthier diet from Karen. And I read a great book called, The China Study, by Dr. Colin Campbell. That study compared American diets with the Chinese and the rest of the world. It showed with a plant-based diet, people do much better in terms of cancer and heart disease. I still like my occasional cheeseburger. Don't get me wrong, it's my favorite food of all time. I once did a sausage commercial for Brown and Serve. But I don't eat those foods as much as I used to.

Bill makes clear that part of the key for him is his running and keeping active:

I once said something like I'd rather have an Olympic gold medal than a million dollars, and that's true. But I also would never quit running. If someone came up to me with a million dollar check and said, "Bill, if you quit running forever and working out and being active, I've got a million to give you." I'd say, "Keep it, you know, and do something good with it." I know what I want to do. I want to run the rest of my life if I can, or at least stay active. But I'm still trying to stay with it, that's the key. . . . I heard this story about DeMar (seven-time winner of the Boston Marathon) when he was in the hospital with cancer. He was still running in the hospital, he's going to make his comeback. I love that story. It's a spiritual sort of thing too. I feel lucky, my cancer is gone. All of us who still have our lives and our health, why should you give it up? Why do you want to give up your health? Don't give it up, it's priceless.

Some advice from Bill: "Take care of yourself. Most Americans don't take care of themselves. Find the activity or sport that you love so you can live your life at your very best. It could be a simple sport like walking or swimming. If you do that, you've got it made."

Parting thoughts from Bill about us old geezers:

There are so many good older runners. And no one knows who they are, and I'm always thinking, God, I wish the media would cover our sport and would take a look at these great American champions, and even older runners from around the world. They're really phenomenal. The sports world is changing, and some of the media gets it and some don't, and I hope your book is an eye opener. . . And I take my hat off to those older runners who inspire almost everybody because they have such great courage.

What the Runners Tell Us

Why Run?

What's the big deal about running anyway? Why do people like to run? It takes such immense effort and you get so easily fatigued. And some people like to go to races and run with such intensity they create stress on their bodies, resulting in pain and discomfort. Why do people put themselves through such suffering? Well, let's take a look at our runners and what they have to say.

Many of these runners took a look at themselves as the years progressed and the pounds increased and thought it was time to take care of their bodies, get some exercise, and take the excess weight off. Most of these individuals made running a part of a healthy lifestyle, a routine discipline that fit in with their busy lives. Furthermore, the fellowship with other runners, and resulting friendships they developed within the running community, were echoed by nearly all featured in this book. Some found after retirement that road racing gave them greater purpose in their lives and more time to devote to the sport. Many runners mention the pleasure of being outside, often surrounded by nature, and the elation of the runner's high as contributing to their feeling of well-being.

The Racing Draw

But why would anyone want to be in a race? To put your body through such punishment, what's the reward? Well, the runners have two words that sum it up: Camaraderie and competition. Those are the ingredients that bring the runner to the starting line, and, once the finish line is crossed, to linger at the refreshment table or go out afterwards with their buddies for breakfast. To many runners the challenge of the race, to contend side by side with the other competitors, to see how they stack up against the field and especially in their age group, is one of the big incentives. Simply put, it's the love to compete. And once the competition is over, it's time for the fun, food, and frolicking with your fellow runners.

Training and Cross-Training

The runners all have their own training methods. Some don't even like calling it training. To them, it is just going out for a run without timing themselves or paying attention to their pace. For others, training is serious business and includes speed work like tempo runs and intervals on a track, running on the hills, and longer easy runs. And there are many shades of gray between these two ends of the spectrum. But there appears to be a pattern: The older they got the more their speed work and mileage were reduced. That doesn't mean, however, that the runners have become any less competitive. Those that thrived on competition earlier in their running careers still seem to bask in that competitive spirit as the years advance.

When it comes to cross-training, there appears to be no definitive consensus. Some of the runners embrace a variety of physical endeavors, often including strength building with weights, swimming, yoga, biking, and hiking. Others adhere strictly to their running and don't seek alternative forms of physical activity. Yet, although the runners themselves appear split on the benefits of cross-training, the use of more muscle groups may, in fact, enhance greater health and vitality as we age.

Starting Later in Life

While there were several elite runners who initiated their racing skills in high school and college and never took much of a break after that, the majority of runners highlighted in this book got off to a late start in life with their running. Most began in their 40s and 50s, many after establishing their careers and having their kids, and a few—like myself—didn't start running until our 60s. Yet, whether they started at 15 or 55, these exceptional athletes continue to astound, running into their 70s, 80s, and several into their 90s, with only a few having to curtail their road racing with great reluctance.

Pushing Beyond the Limits

Although a small percentage of the runners in this book managed somehow to avoid major medical problems, the great majority were—and many still are—battling injuries and other infirmities. This was a constant theme throughout their courageous stories. Their persistence, their perseverance, their "tenacity of spirit," were on full display, and they were not to be denied their love of a sport so endeared to their heart. Several of the runners are cancer survivors who have had major surgeries, and two are still living with cancer; three have had heart attacks, and four have had heart related surgeries; three have had strokes; several have had knee surgeries, and one has had a partial knee replacement; two have had hip replacements—and one of those had both knees done. Only a lucky minority of the runners have dealt with less debilitating maladies, and, consequently, less adverse impact on their ability to run. But here's the amazing thing: Nearly all are still running today.

Lessons Learned

Keys to Their Success, Health, and Longevity

Have these runners given us a prescription to achieve and thrive, to retain our vigor and vitality, and to maintain our well-being into our advanced years? Well, not exactly, but they have given us a template to work with, some discerning messages that could translate a way forward to potentially greater fortune, fitness, and longer life.

Inheritance and Healthy Eating

When it comes to robustness and our bodies, no doubt, there are factors we can control and others we can't. It relates to the old nature-versus-nurture argument and which one has more leverage over our lives. Certainly, genetics holds significant sway over the way we develop and the durability of our physical constitution, an element beyond our human control. A notable number of the runners presented in this book have been gifted with hardy genes from parents who lived well into their 90s and above. On the other hand, there are numerous factors that we can influence. For instance, we have the ability to regulate what and how much we eat. Given our knowledge of nutrition, we have a basic understanding of foods that are healthy and foods to avoid, and most of these runners are cognizant of the difference. They overwhelmingly subscribe to a healthy diet, emphasizing fruits and vegetables, salads, chicken and fish, less meat, and attempting to keep the fast foods and desserts to a minimum.

The Goal, the Race, the Fellowship, the Run, the Blessing

Many of the runners believe that working toward a goal and competing have supplied the impetus for their training and, therefore, are keys for their racing achievements and general well-being. Other runners focus on the sociability at the races, and their running friendships and club affiliations, as motivating factors to keep themselves fit and remain in the sport as long as possible. And most of the runners agree that running and staying physically active are major contributors to their health and longevity. Finally, being blessed, whether by luck or God, was also a frequently mentioned reason for their wellness and living a healthy life.

Advice from the Runners

The runners regularly advised that younger runners ought to heed their warning and not do too much too soon. They suggest these youthful athletes take it slow, build a base, and not go beyond their own capabilities, and in this way avoid the excesses that often lead to injury. It is commonly understood that it takes up to six years of running before you reach your peak in speed and endurance. To the general public, the runner's advice was nearly unanimous: No matter what manner you chose, staying physically active is of the utmost importance for your health. Erika Abraham best illustrates this philosophy when she says: "Drop your technology doohickeys and get off your duff."

Concluding Thoughts from Bill Rodgers

As I've gotten older I believe there's no such thing as an old runner. We're just older runners. Thirty years ago I didn't understand that so much, but as I've gotten older and met so many older runners over the years, I understand that more and more. But I think we're coming into this new era, John, which is sort of the purpose of your book—how you can live your life at your best.

Further Reading

Burfoot, Amby. *The Runners Guide to the Meaning of Life.* New York, NY: Skyhorse, 2007.

Daniels, Jack. *Daniels' Running Formula.* Champaign, IL: Human Kinetics, 2014.

Davidson, Robert. *All Runners Are Crazy.* Barkhamsted, CT: Goulet Printing, 2014.

Dugard, Martin. *To Be a Runner.* New York, NY: Rodale, 2011.

Fixx, Jim. *The Complete Book of Running.* New York, NY: Random House, 1977.

Galloway, Jeff. *Running Until You're 100.* Germany: Meyer & Meyer Sport, 2007.

McDougall, Christopher. *Born to Run.* New York: Vintage Books, A division of Random House, Inc., 2009.

Mipham, Sakyong. *Running with the Mind of Meditation.* New York: Three Rivers Press/Crown Publishing Group, a division of Random House, 2012.

Murakami, Haruki. *What I Talk About When I Talk About Running.* New York: Knopf, 2008.

Rodgers, Bill, and Shepatin, Matthew. *Marathon Man.* New York: St. Martin's Press, 2013.

Sheehan, George. *Running and Being: The Total Experience.* 35th Anniversary Edition. New York: Rodale, 2013.

Switzer, Kathrine and Roger Robinson. *26.2: Marathon Stories.* Toronto, Canada: Madison Press Books produced by Rodale, Inc., 2006.

Van Allen, Jennifer, Bart Yasso, and Amby Burfoot. *The Runner's World: Big Book of Running for Beginners.* New York: Rodale, 2014.